GLORIOUS TRUTHS ABOUT Mother Eve

OTHER BOOKS AND AUDIO BOOKS
BY SUSAN EASTON BLACK

400 Questions and Answers about the Book of Mormon

400 Questions and Answers about the Old Testament

*400 Questions and Answers about the Life
and Times of Jesus Christ*

*400 Questions and Answers about the
Doctrine and Covenants*

Women of Character

Men of Character

GLORIOUS TRUTHS ABOUT *Mother Eve*

SUSAN EASTON BLACK

Covenant Communications, Inc.

Cover image © *The Fall*, after 1479 (oil on panel), Goes, Hugo van der (c.1440-82) / Kunsthistorisches Museum, Vienna, Austria / Bridgeman Images

Cover design copyright © 2018 by Covenant Communications, Inc.
Cover design by Hannah Bischoff

Published by Covenant Communications, Inc.
American Fork, Utah

Copyright © 2018 by Susan Easton Black
All rights reserved. No part of this book may be reproduced in any format or in any medium without the written permission of the publisher, Covenant Communications, Inc., P.O. Box 416, American Fork, UT 84003. This work is not an official publication of The Church of Jesus Christ of Latter-day Saints. The views expressed within this work are the sole responsibility of the author and do not necessarily reflect the position of The Church of Jesus Christ of Latter-day Saints, Covenant Communications, Inc., or any other entity.

Printed in the United States of America
First Printing: March 2018

24 23 22 21 20 19 18   10 9 8 7 6 5 4 3 2 1

ISBN: 978-1-52440-599-1

To Gracie

my beautiful and determined granddaughter

Introduction

"Would you be interested in writing a book on Mother Eve?" Kathy Jenkins asked. The Garden of Eden, a tree laden with fruit, and a serpent-like snake were familiar, but I had questions about the Fall. Why was Eve the first to succumb to Satan's lies and partake of the forbidden fruit? I reasoned that she should have seen deception in the serpent's argument and the downward spiral that would lead from paradise to a mortal world. Rather than give a quick reply to Kathy, my thoughts turned to my own mother.

"Take care of mother" were the last words my father said to me. At the time, my mother was seventy-one, with a blue tint on her graying hair and several aprons neatly tucked in a cupboard. Other than a Cadillac in the garage and discretionary funds to address every whim, mother looked and acted like a typical Mormon housewife of the 1970s. She went to church each week, taught scripture classes in Relief Society, and volunteered occasionally at a thrift shop. She belonged to a book club, a sewing club, and a women's league in town.

Less than a month after Dad passed away, Mother dyed her hair blond, pierced her ears, and entertained a large audience with her rendition of the cancan in a cruise ship talent show. "Take care of mother" did not seem easy now. She was coming out of the home and, in many respects, coming out of a sequestered, if not traditional, lifestyle. She had new friends and new places to go.

The legacy my mother left me is one of embracing the future with all its unknowns and opportunities. Mother died at age ninety-eight. She left a host of friends, all of them much younger than she, and a large posterity who miss her—none more than me. With that in mind and wanting to honor the memory of my mother, I decided to embrace the opportunity to discover truths about Mother Eve. I immersed myself in studies and on more than one occasion was asked by family and friends, "Are you talking about Eve again tonight?" Book after book, consultations with ancient scripture colleagues D. Kelly Ogden and M. Catherine Thomas, and work with research assistants Anna Arts and Eliza A. Allen brought new insights and more questions to consider. There are still issues that I ponder, but what I have discovered about Eve has changed my life. I do not anticipate dyeing my hair blonde, piercing my ears, or dancing the cancan (my readers can tell there is still much for me to learn about life), but I do have a better perceptive of what it means to be a woman.

I invite my readers to discover for themselves the noble role of womanhood in *Glorious Truths about Mother Eve*.

Chapter One

EDEN

FEW COME OF AGE IN our Western culture without knowing something about Mother Eve. Eve, the first woman to be named in holy writ, has become the best-known woman in literature. Bible readers may have trouble recalling that Abraham married Sarai (Sarah) and that Dinah was the sister of Levi, but few hesitate to answer the question, "Who was the help meet of Adam?"

Some wonder, however, whether Eve was the perfect help meet, for she partook of the forbidden fruit and persuaded Adam to do likewise. When Eve's actions in the Garden of Eden are discussed, Mother Eve too often becomes a controversial subject of unfavorable proportions: "Was she a temptress?" "Did she seduce Adam into partaking of the fruit?" "Did she introduce evil into the world?" But before we define Eve by a single episode in Eden, we might want to ask ourselves if we would want to be defined by a single episode in our marriage—or even to have our entire life described on the basis of one decision. What if we were maligned for generations because of one act? Few happily married men would choose a single event to give meaning or definition to their marriage, but such has been the case with Eve.

What happened in the Garden of Eden has become known as the *Eden Narrative*—a straight plot with a defining turning point—and for centuries it has defined Western culture's view of Eve and has even defined the view of the daughters of Eve[1], who weren't even there and who didn't take part in Eve's history-altering decision. It's clear that Eve in one way or another played a critical role in the most ancient story in the world and opened the gate to the conflict between good and evil faced by succeeding generations. Whether hers was an obvious or a subtle choice between right or wrong, many look to Eve as the scapegoat for their own follies or those of others.

Many complex questions surround Eve's choice. Could the struggle on the world front have been avoided if Eve had refused to eat the forbidden fruit? Was the fall of Adam and Eve predetermined, or was it entirely a free choice? Was the Fall of Adam and Eve a step forward or a fall downward? Philosophers continue to grapple with these questions about our first parents. As a result, many label the pivotal role of Eve in the Garden of Eden a sin that characterizes Mother Eve as less than an ideal woman.

Then there is the issue of the scholars' efforts to understand Eve. A great deal of attention has been focused on Eve—as is obvious from a sixty-seven-page bibliography in one monograph about Eden in Hebrew biblical literature.[2] Sorting through the various scholarly interpretations of Eve's role in the Garden of Eden does lead to some insights—but it also shows that some scholars have pushed aside truth in favor of half-truths and even falsehoods.[3]

---

1 Tryggve N. D. Mettinger, *The Eden Narrative: A Literary and Religio-historical Study of Genesis 2-3* (Winona Lake, IN: Eisenbrauns, 2007), 13.

2 See Terje Stordalen, *Echoes of Eden: Genesis 2-3 and Symbolism of the Eden Garden in Biblical Hebrew Literature. Contributions to Biblical Exegesis Theology* (Leuven: Peeters, 2000).

3 Peter Thacher Langer, *Remembering Eden: The Reception History of Genesis 3:22-24* (Oxford: Oxford University Press, 2012), 5.

Some scholars have even gone so far as to justify "women's subordination at creation, her propensity to evil or weakness making her vulnerable to temptation, her responsibility for 'the fall,' and a negative understanding of the word 'helpmeet.'"[4]

In his book *Adam, Who is He?* Elder Mark E. Petersen wrote of the philosophical and scholarly misunderstandings surrounding not only Eve's role in the garden but also Adam's role: "Perhaps no other biblical account has been debated more and understood less than that relating to Adam and Eve. Adam, the first man, is a controversial figure in the minds of many people. So is Eve, his wife. Together, they probably are the most misunderstood couple who ever lived on the earth."[5]

When you consider all the attention the scholarly community has placed on the role of Adam and Eve in the garden, it is surprising that what happened in the garden is not a prominent theme in the Bible or that Eve's partaking of the fruit of the tree of knowledge of good and evil is not used as an example of disobedience or punishment in the Old Testament. This is especially curious in light of a "long story of Israel's recurrent rejection of God's word," which gave ample opportunity for prophetic writers and later philosophers and scholars to discuss what Eve did.[6] There are so few references to Eve in Jewish literature, in fact, that some Hebrew scholars consider the event to be only a "marginal story."[7]

Should we as Latter-day Saints consider Eve as a character in a "marginalized" story? Nothing in Latter-day Saint history

---

4 Marion Ann Taylor and Heather E. Weir, ed., *Let Her Speak for Herself: Nineteenth-Century Women Writing on the Women of Genesis* (Waco, TX: Baylor University Press, 2006), 22.

5 Mark E. Peterson, *Adam, Who is He?* (Salt Lake City: Deseret Book, 1976), 1.

6 Carol Meyers, *Discovering Eve: Ancient Israelite Women in Context* (Oxford: Oxford University Press, 2013), 3.

7 Langer, *Remembering Eden*, 4.

or literature indicates that the story of Eve is a marginal one that can easily be discarded. So let's ask this question: should Latter-day Saints give credence to the more fanciful notion that what we know of Eden is a story of "fictitious heroes or demigods" partaking of fruit from a mythological tree?[8] No; such would be out of harmony with Church doctrines.

Latter-day prophets call Eve "our glorious Mother," and her story is one of sublime womanhood (D&C 138:39). The Prophet Joseph Smith saw in vision Adam[9]—and, according to contemporary Oliver B. Huntington, the Prophet also saw Adam's help meet, Eve.[10] President Brigham Young described "Mother Eve" as having "a splendid influence" over Adam[11]—hardly the disastrous influence so many ascribe to her. Brigham went on to say:

> Some may regret that our first parents sinned. This is nonsense. If we had been there, and they had not sinned, we should have sinned. I will not blame Adam or Eve. Why? Because it was necessary that sin should enter into the world; no man could ever understand the principle of exaltation without its opposite; no one could ever receive an exaltation without being acquainted with its opposite. How did Adam and Eve sin? Did they

---

8 Reverend J. R. Dummelow, *A Commentary on the Holy Bible* (NY: MacMillan, 1908), 1.

9 See Joseph Smith, *History of the Church of Jesus Christ of Latter-day Saints* (Salt Lake City: Deseret Book, 1974), 3:388; D&C 128:21; D&C 107:53–57.

10 Oliver B. Huntington Diary, Part 2, 214, L. Tom Perry Special Collections, Harold B. Lee Library, Brigham Young University, Provo, UT; H. Donl Peterson, *Moroni: Ancient Prophet, Modern Messenger* (Bountiful, UT: Horizon Publishers, 1983), 132–33.

11 Brigham Young, "Traditions, etc.," *Journal of Discourses* 26 vols. (Liverpool: Latter Day Saints' Book Depot, 1855–86), 14:102.

come out in direct opposition to God and to his government? No. But they transgressed a command of the Lord, and through that transgression sin came into the world. The Lord knew they would do this, and he had designed that they should.[12]

President Joseph F. Smith saw in vision the great and mighty who had long since slept, among whom were Adam and Eve. President Smith described Eve as "our glorious Mother Eve" (D&C 138:39). President Russell M. Nelson said of Eve, "We and all mankind are forever blessed because of Eve's great courage and wisdom. By partaking of the fruit first, she did what needed to be done. Adam was wise enough to do likewise."[13] Elder Jeffrey R. Holland said, "To Mother Eve . . . I say, 'Thank you for your crucial role in fulfilling the purposes of eternity.'"[14]

The prophets, then, have confirmed the nobleness of Mother Eve, in stark contrast to what others have interpreted. The words of Latter-day prophets suggest that Eve should not be defamed, but instead enthroned; if we are to believe their words, she should not be demeaned, but revered.

Latter-day Saints Accept Four Accounts of Eve's Story

The first account of Eve's story is recorded in the book of Genesis. The second and third accounts are recorded in the books of Moses and Abraham in The Pearl of Great Price. The fourth account is part

---

12   John A. Widtsoe, *Discourses of Brigham Young, Second President of the Church of Jesus Christ of Latter-day Saints* (Salt Lake City: Deseret Book, 1954), 103.

13   Russell M. Nelson, "Constancy amid Change," *Conference Report*, October 1993.

14   Jeffrey R. Holland, "Behold Thy Mother," *Ensign*, November 2015.

of the temple endowment, where worthy Latter-day Saints learn details about Adam and Eve, the Garden of Eden, their expulsion into mortality, the great plan of salvation, and the Atonement of Jesus Christ. Taken together, the four accounts of Adam and Eve give additional information about truths taught from the beginning—just as the four Gospels (Matthew, Mark, Luke, and John) provide additional information about the mission and ministry of the Savior Jesus Christ.

Let's look more closely at these four accounts.

THE BOOK OF GENESIS ACCOUNT

Genesis means "in the beginning."[15] Genesis actually reveals a sacred record of many beginnings—Creation, man, nature of God, covenants, Israelites, and so on. The most notable of these when it comes to our discussion are the Creation and Adam and Eve.

The Creation is dealt with in just two chapters in Genesis; Adam and Eve's experience in the Garden of Eden and their expulsion into mortality is given even less real estate than that. Compare the scanty information about Adam and Eve to other accounts in Genesis: the span from the expulsion from Eden to Father Abraham is recorded in eight chapters in Genesis. The story of Abraham is presented in about a dozen chapters, while the stories of Isaac, Jacob, Joseph, and the founding of the house of Israel are recorded in twenty-four chapters.[16] In terms of word count alone, the Genesis text has more information about the patriarchal order and teachings of the patriarchs than it does about the Creation or the story of Adam and Eve. Putting it

---

15 Dummelow, *Commentary on the Holy Bible*, 1.

16 Robert J. Matthews, "The Old Testament: A Voice from the Past and a Witness for the Lord Jesus Christ," in *Sperry Symposium Classics: Old Testament* (Provo, UT: Religious Studies Center, 2005), 41.

another way, out of the 929 chapters in the Old Testament, only 24 are *not* about Jacob and his posterity. (These totals do not take into account that Job may not have been an Israelite or that the book of Ecclesiastes is not about Jacob and his posterity.)

Yet the first few chapters of Genesis—the prologue to the story of the patriarchs—is of primary importance to people throughout the world; that's where we find information about the Creation, and it's where we read the story of our first parents. Genesis begins with the Creation, moves to Adam and Eve, and ends with a mummy—Joseph of Egypt in a coffin. Lest it appear that from Creation to the mummy is a slippery, downward slope for all mankind, "implicit in the end is a promise of more life to come, of irrepressible procreation, and that renewal of creation will be manifested."[17] Also, the pages between the creation of heaven and earth and the coffin contain "some of the most memorable and moving narratives within the Old Testament."[18] These narratives have captured the hearts and minds of the Lord's children throughout the ages. These stories have also given literature and art images that have placed Genesis ahead of the other thirty-eight books in the Old Testament in influence and recognition.[19]

With all that, our first parents are written as if they were "minor characters in Genesis, a book dominated by the grand Epic of the House of Abraham—a narrative with the grandeur and span of an *Iliad* or an *Odyssey.*"[20] Although Adam and Eve and their offspring—Cain, Abel, and Seth—pass by in rapid succession "to a narrative which finds its rhythm when Abraham

---

17   Robert Alter, *Genesis: Translation and Commentary* (NY and London: W. W. Norton and Co., 1996), xlvi.

18   R. W. L. Moberly, *The Theology of the Book of Genesis* (Cambridge, England: Cambridge University Press, 2009), 1.

19   Moberly, *Theology of the Book of Genesis*, 1.

20   Moberly, *Theology of the Book of Genesis*, 1.

sets out on his way from Mesopotamia to Palestine," Adam and Eve are the foundation narrative in Genesis that sets the tone for the Old Testament.[21]

The Book of Moses Account

Selections from the book of Moses contain a fuller account of the Creation and the story of Adam and Eve than what is in the Genesis text. Because of that, the book of Moses is viewed by Latter-day Saints as a prelude to Genesis.[22] We are blessed to have that account for many reasons, not the least of which is the insight it gives us into Eve and the intents of her heart.

The Prophet Joseph Smith began his revision of Genesis in June 1830 in fulfillment of the Lord's promise, "In a day when the children of men shall esteem my words as naught and take many of them from the book which thou shalt write, behold, I will raise up another like unto [Moses]; and they shall be had again among the children of men—among as many as shall believe" (Moses 1:41). Joseph Smith's purpose in revising Genesis was to clarify and restore important truths of history and doctrine missing from the biblical text.

The book of Moses begins, "The words of God, which he spake unto Moses at a time when Moses was caught up into an exceedingly high mountain" (Moses 1:1). As we read this inspired text, we learn that Moses saw in vision the organization of this earth and that he recorded his vision sometime before the Israelite exodus from Egypt.[23] Chapter 1 tells of God revealing Himself to Moses, showing him worlds (seemingly without number), and revealing the fallen state of Lucifer. Succeeding chapters show

---

21   See J. H. H. Weiler, "God's Serpent (Genesis 2-3)," in Beth Kissileff, ed., *Reading Genesis: Beginnings* (London: Bloomsbury, 2016), 43–56.

22   See *Old Testament: Gospel Doctrine Teacher's Supplement* (Salt Lake City: The Church of Jesus Christ of Latter-day Saints, 1985), 8.

23   *Old Testament: Gospel Doctrine Teacher's Supplement*, 10.

the Lord's interactions with Adam and Eve and their posterity following their expulsion from the Garden of Eden—something that is only briefly touched on in the book of Genesis.[24]

Even if there was nothing more than that in the book of Moses, it would be a lost treasure worthy of inclusion in The Pearl of Great Price. But there *is* more! The book of Moses reveals that Adam and Eve came to understand the atoning sacrifice of Jesus Christ and the plan of salvation (see Moses 6:51–63). The book of Moses tells us that the sacrificial offerings of Adam and Eve were "a similitude of the sacrifice of the Only Begotten of the Father" (Moses 5:7). The book of Moses reveals that Adam was baptized in water, received the gift of the Holy Ghost, and knew the purpose of the Fall (see Moses 5:9; 6:64–68). And just look what it tell us about Eve's role in the Fall: the book of Moses tells us that Eve beautifully exclaimed, "Were it not for our transgression we never should have had seed, and never should have known good and evil, and the joy of our redemption, and the eternal life which God giveth unto all the obedient" (Moses 5:11).

The Book of Abraham Account

On July 3, 1835, Michael H. Chandler, a traveling entrepreneur from Pennsylvania, came to Kirtland, Ohio, to exhibit four Egyptian mummies "together with some two or more rolls of papyrus covered with hieroglyphic figures and devises."[25] The Prophet Joseph Smith wrote, "Mr. Chandler had been told I could translate the figures on the papyrus and give him an interpretation."[26] Indeed he could. Two days later—on July 5, 1835—Joseph Smith

---

24 See Bruce T. Taylor, "Book of Moses," in Daniel H. Ludlow, ed., *Encyclopedia of Mormonism* (NY: Macmillan, 1992), 216–17.

25 George Reynolds, "The Book of Abraham—It's Genuineness Established," *Latter Day Saints' Millennial Star* 41, no. 1 (January 6, 1879), 2.

26 Smith, *History of the Church*, 2:236.

"commenced the translation of some of the characters or hieroglyphics, and much to our joy found that one of the rolls contained the writings of Abraham, another the writings of Joseph of Egypt, etc." Joseph then wrote, "Truly we can say, the Lord is beginning to reveal the abundance of peace and truth."[27]

The book of Abraham contains a brief recounting of Abraham's experiences in Chaldea, Haran, Canaan, and Egypt as well as a vision given to Abraham through the Urim and Thummim. In the vision, Abraham saw glimpses of worlds, premortal spirits, a council in heaven, and the Creation of the world. But it is what we learn about the Creation that may be the most pivotal part of the book.

As Joseph Smith translated the Abrahamic writings, he discovered that Abraham's account of the Creation differed from the account recorded in the book of Moses and from the account recorded in Genesis. President Joseph Fielding Smith explained why: "Abraham gives an account of the planning in heaven for this earth and its inhabitants, before the work of building was done. I do not say that this planning contemplated the creation of the sun or other heavenly bodies, but rather the placing of the earth in the position which it was to occupy in relation to these orbs." President Smith concluded, "The account of the creation of the earth as given in Genesis, and the Book of Moses, and as given in the temple, is the creation of the physical earth, and of physical animals and plants."[28]

As Joseph Smith continued to translate the book of Abraham, he read of Adam being placed in the Garden of Eden "to dress and keep it" (Abraham 5:11). He also read of a woman, of whom Adam declared, "This was bone of my bones, and flesh of my

---

27   Smith, *History of the Church*, 2:236.

28   Joseph Fielding Smith, *Doctrines of Salvation: Sermons and Writings of Joseph Fielding Smith* 4 vols. (Salt Lake City: Bookcraft, 1954), 1:75.

flesh; now she shall be called Woman, because she was taken out of man" (Abraham 5:17). Abraham concludes his account by explaining that the woman was "an help meet" for Adam (Abraham 5:21). With this account, we realize in an entirely new way the glorious purpose and role Eve was to play.

THE TEMPLE ACCOUNT
Due to the sacred nature of the Adam and Eve story as presented in the endowment, we can't discuss it in detail here. Any who have attended the temple know that the sacred roles of both Adam and Eve and the plan of salvation are presented with great clarity within those hallowed walls. President Henry B. Eyring stated, "In the temple you will learn more about the Creation of the world, about the patterns in the lives of Adam and Eve, and most importantly, about our Savior, Jesus Christ."[29]

OTHER ACCOUNTS OF EVE'S STORY
Although Latter-day Saints turn to Genesis, Moses, Abraham, and the temple for insights into the life and choices of Eve, there are other lesser-known accounts of her story. We look forward with anticipation to the translation of the plates of brass, which contain a "genealogy of our forefathers, even from the beginning" (Alma 37:3). Surely they will have insights into Eve that we have not yet learned.

In addition to the plates of brass, there are other accounts of Eve among the Greeks, Syrians, Egyptians, and Hebrews,[30] though these are far less known to Latter-day Saints. For example, Eve is mentioned in the Apocryphal literature of Tobit 8:6; Sirach 25:24, 40:1, 42:13; and 4 Maccabees 18:7.[31]

---

29 Henry B. Eyring, "Man Down!" *Conference Report*, April 2009.
30 Rutherford H. Platt Jr., ed., *The Forgotten Books of Eden, the Apocrypha, Forbidden and Lost Books of the Bible* (Cleveland, OH: World Publishing Company, 1927), 3.
31 Taylor and Weir, *Let Her Speak for Herself*, 22.

In the *Forgotten Books of Eden*, author Rutherford H. Platt includes the text of an unknown Egyptian or Egyptians whose writings in Arabic were translated into Ethiopic.[32] Our greatest interest in this two-part work is the First Book of Adam and Eve, which begins where the Genesis story of Adam and Eve leaves off. This account informs readers of the "careers of Adam and Eve, from the day they left Eden; their dwelling in the Cave of Treasures; their trials and temptations; [and] Satan's manifold apparitions to them. The birth of Cain, of Abel, and of their twin sisters; Cain's love for his own twin sister, Luluwa, whom Adam and Eve wished to join to Abel; the details of Cain's murder of his brother; and Adam's sorrow and death."[33] President Russell M. Nelson said of this text:

> While visiting the British Museum in London one day, I read a most unusual book. It is not scripture. It is an English translation of an ancient Egyptian manuscript. From it, I quote a dialogue between the Father and the Son. Referring to His Father, Jehovah—the premortal Lord—says: "He took the clay from the hand of the angel, and made Adam according to Our image and likeness, and He left him lying for forty days and forty nights without putting breath into him. And He heaved sighs over him daily, saying, 'If I put breath into this [man], he must suffer many pains.' And I said unto My Father, 'Put breath into him; I will be an advocate for him.' And My Father said unto Me, 'If I put breath into him, My beloved Son, Thou wilt be obliged to go

---

32   Platt, *Forgotten Books of Eden*, 3.
33   Platt, *Forgotten Books of Eden*, 4.

down into the world, and to suffer many pains for him before Thou shalt have redeemed him, and made him to come back to his primal state.' And I said unto My Father, 'Put breath into him; I will be his advocate, and I will go down into the world, and will fulfil Thy command.'"[34]

Although the ancient text is not scripture, President Nelson affirmed it "teach[es] of the deep and compassionate love of the Father for the Son, and of the Son for us—attesting that Jesus volunteered willingly to be our Savior and Redeemer."[35]

Books of scripture accepted by members of other faiths also refer to Eve. In the Quran, the central text of Islam, the name of Eve is *Hawwa*, which comes from the root word *hay*, meaning "living." The Quran states, "And God said: 'O Mankind! Be dutiful to your Lord, Who created you from a single person (Adam) and from Him (Adam) He created his wife (Eve), and from them both He created many men and women'" (Quran 4:1). The Quran describes Adam and Eve living in tranquility in paradise until Satan deceives them by saying, "Your Lord did not forbid you this tree save that you should become Angels or become of the immortals" (Quran 7:20).

In the New Testament, Eve is mentioned only twice—both in the writings of the Apostle Paul. In 1 Timothy, Paul writes, "But I suffer not a woman to teach, nor to usurp authority over the man, but to be in silence. For Adam was first formed, then Eve. And Adam was not deceived, but the woman being deceived was in the transgression" (1 Timothy 2:12–14). In 2 Corinthians, he writes, "But I fear, lest by any means, as the serpent beguiled Eve through his subtilty, so your minds should be corrupted from the

---

34 Russell M. Nelson, "The Creation," *Conference Report*, April 2000.
35 Nelson, "The Creation," *Conference Report*, April 2000.

simplicity that is in Christ" (2 Corinthians 11:3). These writings of Paul reinforce the concept that Eve was deceived and beguiled.

Then there are accounts of Adam and Eve in what are called "extra-biblical works"—the most famous being John Milton's epic poem *Paradise Lost* (1667). In Milton's work, Adam is depicted as more perfect than Eve, for he more closely resembles God. Yet he has a weakness for Eve, as shown in Milton's description of the "Fall from Grace":

> Of man's first disobedience, and the fruit
> Of that forbidden tree, whose mortal taste
> Brought death into the world, and all our woe,
> With loss of Eden, till one greater man
> Restore us, and regain the blissful seat,
> Sing Heav'nly Muse. . . .
> What in me is dark
> Illumine, what is low raise and support;
> That to the heighth of this great argument
> I may assert Eternal Providence,
> And justify the ways of God to men.[36]

Milton then pits Adam and Eve against each other in a petty exchange of blame for the "Fall from Grace." In Milton's work, Eve takes the brunt of the blame because her heart had accepted the enticing of Satan.[37]

Since Milton's remarkable literary work, there have been many other mentions of Eden outside the Bible, but none have

---

36 See Barbara Lewalski, ed., *John Milton Paradise Lost* (Victoria, Australia: Blackwell Publishing, 2007).

37 See John S. Tanner, *Anxiety in Eden: A Kierkegaardian Reading of Paradise Lost* (New York, Oxford: Oxford University Press, 1992).

had the time-honored influence of *Paradise Lost*.[38] Yet that hasn't stopped poets or religionists from putting forth interpretations, misconceptions, and even far-out theories about Adam and Eve in Eden. As Latter-day Saints, our responsibility is to find within scripture and the words of the Lord's prophets insight into the heart and mind of Eve, whose greatest desire was to be a righteous servant to the Lord and help meet to her husband.

---

[38] N. Eldon Tanner, "Warnings from Outer Space," *Conference Report*, October 1972.

Chapter Two

INTERPRETING EVE

It's not hard to imagine a tree laden with fruit or a serpent-like snake. We can *see* them in our mind's eye, yet when it comes to discussing the symbolic meaning behind these significant images in the Garden of Eden, too often it's difficult to agree on exactly what they *mean*.[1] The varying opinions on what they mean can ultimately be traced to the works of early Church fathers and philosophers who studied events in the Garden of Eden based only on what they knew and learned from the book of Genesis.

Looking for hidden truths and meaning in the symbols, these learned men reached conclusions that varied widely. Most early philosophers held fast to what they read in the book of Genesis, accepting no variations from what they interpreted as the word of God. Others suggested that the Genesis text was a reference point for their interpretation, but that it certainly didn't overshadow

---

1   Joseph Abraham, *Eve: Accused or Acquitted? An Analysis of Feminist Readings of the Creation Narrative in Texts in Genesis 1-3*, Paternoster Biblical Monographs (Eugene, OR: Wipf and Stock, 2002), 56.

their own works. Still others claimed that the series of events presented in the book of Genesis was a myth.

So how do we peel back centuries of interpretations so we can discover the sacred truth about the character of Eve? Such an effort would be almost impossible if we didn't have the words of latter-day prophets.

Interpretations of Eve

Most interpretations of what happened in the garden portray Mother Eve as less than an ideal help meet for Adam. Partaking of the forbidden fruit and inviting Adam to do likewise has not only cast a long shadow over Eve's reputation, but has sullied the reputations of generations of women. Because of that, ancient Hebrew interpreters justified themselves in imposing "rules of conduct that applied to the most intimate details of women's life."[2] Biblical scholar Nehama Aschkenasy said that such restrictions might have been less cruel had their reach not been so exhaustive:

> The woman became the chattel of [the] male, part of his worldly possessions, and she lost her freedom to choose and decide for herself. In biblical times, women of childbearing age were constantly confined in the home, tending to the children and domestic matters. The socio-economic realities were such that a person's worth was measured by his or her labor input. Consequently, female children were less desirable than male children, since they were not able to offer the same manpower to the family as the male children.[3]

---

2 Nehama Aschkenasy, *Eve's Journey: Feminine Images in Hebraic Literary Tradition* (Philadelphia: University of Pennsylvania Press, 1986), 8.

3 Aschkenasy, *Eve's Journey*, 109.

She said that under the patriarchal system, "The responsibility for supporting the family was man's, but this created a male-dominated unit in which the woman was economically . . . dependent on her father and later, on her husband. A woman's earnings belonged to her husband, and she did not share in her father's estate." She then concludes, "If the Bible cannot be blamed for conspiring to subjugate women, its male-dominated laws inevitably perpetuated the image of women as subordinate to the male and inferior to him."[4]

Muslim sources also mention this negative interpretation of a woman's place in the patriarchal structure of Judaism. They claim that "until the present day, orthodox Jewish men in their daily morning prayer recite 'Blessed be God King of the universe that Thou has not made me a woman.'"[5] These same sources quote from a Jewish prayer book: "Praised be God that he has not created me a gentile. Praised be God that he has not created me a woman. Praised be God that he has not created me an ignoramus."[6]

You might scoff at this kind of reasoning and propaganda, but there is evidence to support some of the conclusions. In one ancient rabbinical text, the question is asked, "Why does the woman walk in front of the corpse at a funeral, and why was the precept of menstruation given to her?" The answer is that "[Eve] shed the blood of Adam" by giving him fruit of the tree of the knowledge of good and evil, which brought death to man. The book then asks, as

---

4 Aschkenasy, *Eve's Journey*, 109.

5 Abu Abdur Rahman Faruq Post, comp., *Best Women on the Face of the Earth: Clarification of How True Believing Muslim Women are the Best of Women* (Dar uf Itabaa Publications, 2013), 10.

6 Michael J. Wilkins, *The New Matthew Application Commentary: From Biblical Text to Contemporary Life* (Grand Rapids, MI: Zondervan, 1973), 920.

if in a run-on sentence, "Why was the precept of the dough (*hallah*) given to her?" The answer—"[Eve] corrupted Adam, who was the dough of the world," a reference to his being created out of the "dust of the ground" (Genesis 2:7). Continuing, it then asks, "Why was the precept of the Sabbath lights given to her?" Unfortunately, the answer is because "she extinguished the soul of Adam."[7]

In the Jewish *Mishnah*, rabbis say that the woman is "an object of study and exploration, an entity apart from the male world, the latter being the norm of the human condition."[8] This is followed by curses inflicted on all women because Eve was the first to partake of the forbidden fruit—curses including "the burden of the blood of menstruation and the blood of virginity; the burden of pregnancy; the burden of childbirth; the burden of bringing up the children; her head is covered as one in mourning; she pierces her ear like a permanent slave or slave girl who serves her master; she is not to be believed as a witness; and after everything—death."[9]

Perhaps popular Christian interpretation isn't much better. One Christian scholar claims that the fact that Eve partook of the forbidden fruit first is "pivotal to the whole Christian faith because the Christian conception of the reason for the mission of Jesus Christ on Earth stems from Eve's disobedience to God."[10] Christians are taught that Eve seduced Adam into partaking of the fruit—and that she was the direct cause of them being expelled from the Garden of Eden. Putting the issue in a more straightforward way, Christians are taught, "Eve is responsible for her own mistake, her husband's sin, the original sin of all

---

7   *Genesis Rabbah*, 17:8; Aschkenasy, *Eve's Journey*, 3.
8   Aschkenasy, *Eve's Journey*, 8.
9   Post, *Best Women on the Face of the Earth*, 10.
10 Sherif Muhammad Abdel Azeem, *Women in Islam vs. Women in Judaeo-Christian Tradition: Myth & Reality* (Raleigh, NC: Lulu Press, 2013), 8.

humanity, and the death of the Son of God. In other words, one woman acting on her own caused the fall of humanity."[11]

That Christian view blames Eve for evil, justifying it by concluding, "She is the one who first surrendered to temptation and violated God's law."[12] But they don't stop there. Early Christian fathers not only saw evil in Eve's actions but professed that all women "inherited from their mother, the Biblical Eve, both her guilt and her guile. Consequently, they were all untrustworthy, morally inferior, and wicked. Menstruation, pregnancy, and childbearing were considered the just punishment for the eternal guilt of the cursed female sex."[13]

How did Christians—followers of the merciful Christ—come to interpret Eve in such a negative way? The simplistic answer is that most orthodox Christians agreed with their Jewish contemporaries who believed that Eve's misuse of freedom or agency followed by Adam's partaking of the forbidden fruit "brought pain, labor, and death into an originally perfect world."[14]

Take for example Philo of Alexandria, who warned fellow Christians "against women, whose creation from Adam's side ended the first man's lofty and solitary communion with God." Philo claimed the actions of Eve were "the beginning of all evils." Yet Philo also interpreted the story of Adam and Eve as if it were a myth rather than the word of God. Even so, he said the Eden story was filled with profound truths hidden in symbols.[15] To Philo, Adam and Eve represent elements of human nature—Adam the

---

11 Azeem, *Women in Islam vs. Women in Judaeo-Christian Tradition*, 8.

12 Aschkenasy, *Eve's Journey*, 39.

13 Azeem, *Women in Islam vs. Women in Judaeo-Christian Tradition*, 7.

14 Elaine H. Pagels, *Adam, Eve, and the Serpent: Sex and Politics in Early Christianity* (Toronto: Random House, 1988), 73.

15 See F. H. Colson and G. H. Whitaker, *Philo, Volume 1* 10 vols. (Cambridge, MA: Harvard University Press, 1981).

"mind (*nous*), the nobler, masculine, and rational element, which is 'made in God's image,'" and Eve represented "the body or sensation (*aisthesis*), the lower, feminine element, source of all passion."[16]

Others were even more direct than Philo in condemning Eve. In speaking to sisters of the Christian faith, Quintus Septimius Forens Tertullian asked,

> Do you not know that you are each an Eve? The sentence of God on this sex of yours lives in this age: the guilt must of necessity live too. You are the Devil's gateway: You are the unsealer of the forbidden tree: You are the first deserter of the divine law: You are she who persuaded him whom the devil was not valiant enough to attack. You destroyed so easily God's image, man.[17]

Although such false interpretations are monstrous in their implications for Eve and women in general, there were few early Church fathers with enough courage to stand up for Mother Eve. Origen Adamantius (185–254 AD) surely lacked that courage. In his monumental thirteen volume *Commentary on Genesis* (only a few segments of which have survived due in large part to being condemned in the sixth century), Origen condemns Mother Eve for all eternity.[18] Another early Christian theologian and philosopher—Augustine, the bishop of Hippo (354–430

---

16 Pagels, *Adam, Eve, and the Serpent*, 64–65.

17 S. Thelwall, translator, "Tertullian: On the Apparel of Women," in Alexander Roberts and James Donaldson, ed., *The Ante-Nicene Fathers* (NY: Christian Literature Company, 1890), 4:14; Azeem, *Women in Islam vs. Women in Judaeo-Christian Tradition*, 8.

18 Peter W. Martens, "A Fitting Portrait of God: Origen's Interpretations of the 'Garments of Skins' (Gen. 3:21)," in Caroline Vander and Susanne Scholz, ed., *Hidden Truths from Eden: Esoteric Readings of Genesis 1-3* (Atlanta: Society of Biblical Literature, Semeia Studies, no. 76, 2014), 55.

AD)—supported the theory of "original sin."[19] He went so far as to say that the consequence of partaking of the forbidden fruit was sin, guilt, and depravity that were then passed on to the posterity of Adam and Eve. Standing up for Eve was dangerous; when philosopher Flavius Claudius Julianus (330–361 AD) disagreed on all fronts with Augustine, he was pronounced a heretic.[20] Augustine wrote to a friend, "What is the difference whether it is in a wife or a mother, it is still Eve the temptress that we must beware of in any woman. . . . I fail to see what use woman can be to man, if one excludes the function of bearing children."[21]

Initially, the theory of original sin was adopted by only small groups of Christians who spoke of it as the "doctrine" of original sin—even a doctrine of truth.[22] But by the late fourth and early fifth century, the doctrine of original sin had been embraced as mainstream Christian belief.[23] You might wonder how such an interpretation of Genesis could become so embraced—but maybe a quote from nineteenth-century poet William Blake (1757–1827) says it best: "Both read the Bible day and night; but you read black where I read white!"[24] Today millions of Catholics and Protestants believe the story of Adam and Eve as "virtually synonymous with original sin."[25]

---

19 N. P. Williams, *The Ideas of the Fall and of Original Sin: A Historical and Critical Study* (London: Longmans, Green, 1927), 327–28.

20 Pagels, *Adam, Eve, and the Serpent*, 143.

21 Gillian Cloke, *This Female Man of God: Women and Spiritual Power in the Patristic Age, AD 350-450* (London and NY: Routledge, 1995), 95; Azeem, *Women in Islam vs. Women in Judaeo-Christian Tradition*, 8.

22 See Douglas S. Ladle, "Teaching the Fall of Adam and Eve," in *Religious Educator* 5, no. 1 (2004): 41–55; Pagels, *Adam, Eve, and the Serpent*, 126.

23 Moberly, *Theology of the Book of Genesis*, 77.

24 Pagels, *Adam, Eve, and the Serpent*, 62; see Janine Dehn, *Analysis "Garden of Love" by William Blake* (Norderstedt, Germany: Grim, 2006).

25 Pagels, *Adam, Eve, and the Serpent*, xxvi.

Results of Such Interpretations

We can surely tell the truth about the garden, the tree, the fruit, and the serpent—but can that truth be believed? We might think the answer is obvious—but in reality, interpretive reading or misreading of the story of Adam and Eve has practically become scripture all on its own. For example, mistaken interpretations of the Genesis text are responsible for the commonly held belief that men are superior to women, which leads to the conclusion that women are inferior to men. (This author has never met an inferior woman.)

Then there is the erroneous conclusion that woman was created to be a "helpmate, a lower-order companion to stave off male loneliness."[26] Such an unfounded, unscriptural belief should be repugnant to any Christian who worships a God of love. It is especially offensive when coupled with the notion that because the woman tempted Adam with the forbidden fruit, she is therefore "responsible for all human sinfulness."[27]

Take a close look at the questions such a theory necessarily causes. Would the Lord condemn Eve as a scapegoat for all the evil in the world? Would the Lord curse all His daughters because Eve was the first to eat of the forbidden fruit? Would the Lord damn His daughters to be inferior to men from one generation to the next? Would the God of heaven, the God of the universe, the God of love want His daughters demeaned in any way? Would he want Mother Eve, that most glorious woman, mocked and cursed throughout time and eternity?

The answers to those questions are so obvious. But that doesn't stop philosophers, sages, and theologians from hurling slurs on Eve or her daughters. Using Mother Eve as a model or pattern, they contend that all women must be suppressed by

---

26 Meyers, *Discovering Eve*, 78.
27 Meyers, *Discovering Eve*, 78.

wiser and superior male figures.[28] The way they look at Eve violates the very reason Adam and Eve were placed in the garden. The effect of their damning words refutes the "integrity, rhetoric, lexical choices, and cultural setting" of Christianity and the holy garden scene.[29] Claiming that the Genesis text "deliberately promotes male dominion and female subordination" doesn't just miss the mark—it is an affront to God, to the plan of salvation, and to women.[30]

That's not all. When people speak of "prophetesses and extraordinary female characters" as the exception in the Bible, they "illuminate the inferior position of the majority of women in the biblical culture."[31] Writing that biblical women are seldom cast in a central role, that masses of anonymous women come across as restrained and nonverbal, that they in fact lack ability to articulate and express themselves, and that they have little to no creative imagination results in a never-ending litany of scriptural-based put-downs for women.[32] Since the majority of women in holy writ are anonymous ("even those who are named, like Dinah, are not always given the opportunity to express their voice"), Christian scholars have found precious little reason to reconsider their interpretation of Eve or her daughters.[33]

The reasoning of these scholars has spilled over into Western society and has served as the basis for shaping Western attitudes about gender, identity, and the role of women in marriage, family life, and society.[34] As a result, many women in Western

---

28 Meyers, *Discovering Eve*, 76.
29 Meyers, *Discovering Eve*, 79.
30 Aschkenasy, *Eve's Journey*, 9.
31 Aschkenasy, *Eve's Journey*, 10.
32 Aschkenasy, *Eve's Journey*, 162.
33 Aschkenasy, *Eve's Journey*, 161.
34 Meyers, *Discovering Eve*, preface.

society have taken a back seat to the dominant male, not only by tradition but in life. According to Aschkenasy, "Women have played the role of the 'other' for men; whether they were put on a pedestal as a symbol of virtue and nobility, or blamed as the originators of death and sin in this world, women were not allowed to epitomize the entire human experience."[35]

If you are prone to disagree with this interpretive glance at Eve and her daughters, reread John Milton's *Paradise Lost*. His remarkable and influential tale about Eden has so strongly implanted his interpretation of Eve on Western culture that "many of our present recollections of the biblical story are more faithful to his portrayal of Eve or Satan" than to what the original writers of the Bible text intended.[36] In *Paradise Lost*—

> Eve emerges as childishly irresponsible, susceptible to flattery, and predisposed to evil. Her vicious and jealous nature is revealed when she vacillates between offering the fruit to Adam and withholding it from him. If her mental capacities have indeed been augmented as a result of eating from the tree of knowledge, so she reasons, then by sharing the fruit with Adam she runs the risk of making him as wise as she has become. If God's threat was real, however, and she has become mortal as a result of her violation of His command, then by keeping the fruit away from her mate she would enable him to survive her and marry another woman. By contrast, Adam's motives for tasting from the forbidden fruit are purely noble: he would rather die than live without Eve.[37]

---

35 Aschkenasy, *Eve's Journey*, 7.
36 Meyers, *Discovering Eve*, 76.
37 Aschkenasy, *Eve's Journey*, 39.

Rather than give Milton the final word on Eve, many have reexamined the actions of Eve in the garden. As they assess Eve's role in the garden, traditional interpretations of the Adam and Eve story against the backdrop of modern society have begun to erode since the 1970s—"the decade of the woman."[38]

Never before or since the 1970s has so much been said or written about women's role and place in Western society. Traditional thinkers trumpeted woman's role as unchanging: like her mother, grandmother, and female ancestors for millennia, the ideal woman was a mother nurturing the rising generation in the home and living with the consequences of "original sin." Feminists rebelled and labeled that traditional role as stereotypical, confining, and demeaning. Their solution to the problems that had troubled women for centuries was the Equal Rights Amendment (ERA), which stated "equality of rights under the law shall not be denied or abridged by the United States or by any State on account of sex."

Members of The Church of Jesus Christ of Latter-day Saints spoke out loudly on both sides of the ERA, even after Church leaders referred to the proposed amendment as a danger to the time-honored moral values that safeguarded womanhood and the sanctity of the family.[39] By March 1973, thirty of the thirty-eight states needed to ratify the ERA had voted to legalize the proposed amendment. Utah, Arizona, and Nevada—each with a dense population of Latter-day Saint women—were still waiting to be polled.

In this period of moral uncertainty, feminist authors delved into the Genesis text and early Jewish and Christian sources to uncover "the cultural and mythical roots in which misogyny is embedded" and to cry wolf over what they perceived as a "deliberate strategy on the part of the biblical lawmaker and storyteller to

---

38   Meyers, *Discovering Eve*, 6–7.
39   See "The Church and the Proposed Equal Rights Amendment: A Moral Issue," *Ensign*, March 1980.

perpetuate male dominance and female subjugation."[40] Feminists distorted the Genesis text to defend Eve and to suggest that her partaking of the forbidden fruit was a "'fall upwards' into freedom."[41]

Although their distorted interpretation had elements of truth, the context in which their conclusions were reached is questioned. Feminists portrayed Eve as an intellectually curious woman whose quest for knowledge "led to human civilization as we know it"—man and woman making clothes, tilling the ground, bearing and rearing children, and so on. Feminists concluded that "there is no indication in the original story that Adam is perceived as superior to Eve in any way; man and woman are equally culpable in the eyes of God, and equally responsible for the consequences of their deed."[42]

Feminists raised Eve to heights never before depicted in the literature, but in so doing demeaned Adam to an insufferable low. Feminist authors portrayed Adam as a passive character who slept while the woman was being formed, who followed Eve blindly by partaking of the forbidden fruit, and who blamed the woman when God asked him, "Hast thou eaten of the tree, whereof I commanded thee that thou shouldest not eat?" (Genesis 3:11)

Prophets Speak of Eve

We have been counseled to follow the direction of our modern-day prophets—so we need to ask where they stand in relation to the story of Adam and Eve. The answer is simple. Latter-day prophets denounce all interpretations and teachings of the Eden story that suggest negative views of Eve; they likewise decry the

---

40   Aschkenasy, *Eve's Journey*, 9.

41   Paul Morris and Deborah Sawyer, ed., *A Walk in the Garden: Biblical, Iconographical and Literary Images in Eden* (London: Bloomsbury Publishing and T. & T. Clark, 1992), 144.

42   Aschkenasy, *Eve's Journey*, 11.

feminist views that deride the character of Adam. For example, the Prophet Joseph Smith denounced the theory of original sin in one simple sentence: "We believe that men will be punished for their own sins, and not for Adam's transgression" (Articles of Faith 2).

Joseph Smith did not bury this sentence deep in the Articles of Faith or even put it at the end of his statements of belief. Instead, the Prophet Joseph placed it second, next to the professed belief in "God, the Eternal Father, and in His Son, Jesus Christ, and in the Holy Ghost" (Articles of Faith 1). The Prophet Joseph's announcement that man is not punished for Adam's transgression overturns in an instant a major tenet held sacred by the Christian world. Early philosophers and Christian leaders would surely denounce Joseph Smith as a false prophet and a heretic for that one sentence alone. But none of the texts written by early Christian leaders or today's feminists change the truth. As Elder M. Russell Ballard stated, "The Church of Jesus Christ of Latter-day Saints discounts the notion of Original Sin and its ascribed negative impact on humanity."[43]

There is little wiggle room or vagueness in the statements of the Prophet Joseph Smith or Elder M. Russell Ballard. These inspired prophetic men are not like Tevye in *Fiddler on the Roof*, who turns again and again to tradition for answers. Neither do they mirror Tevye as he repeats the phrase "on the other hand" when he learns of his daughter's engagement to the tailor Hodel. To holy prophets, when it comes to the story of Adam and Eve there is *no other hand*, for never will man or woman be punished for Adam's transgression.

The unwavering prophetic interpretation of the ancient story of the tree, fruit, and serpent should cause the Christian world to

---

43 M. Russell Ballard, *Our Search for Happiness: An Invitation to Understand The Church of Jesus Christ of the Latter-day Saints* (Salt Lake City: Deseret Book, 1993), 86.

stand up and listen, for the shackles of oppression on women have fallen—cast aside by revealed truth.[44] To fancy that Eve's taste of the forbidden fruit has tainted women and created second-class citizens in society is as wrong as continuing to view Eve through the distorted lenses of Jewish and Christian tradition. President Dallin H. Oaks has said, "Some Christians condemn Eve for her act, concluding that she and her daughters are somehow flawed by it. Not the Latter-day Saints! Informed by revelation, we celebrate Eve's act and honor her wisdom and courage in the great episode called the Fall."[45]

"I never speak of the part Eve took in this fall as a sin, nor do I accuse Adam of a sin," wrote President Joseph Fielding Smith. "This was a transgression of the law, but not a sin . . . for it was something that Adam and Eve had to do!"[46] The action of Eve in the Garden of Eden was a central part of the plan of salvation. In the clear light of revelation, the actions of Mother Eve are celebrated, not condemned.

---

44   Meyers, *Discovering Eve*, 87.
45   Dallin H. Oaks, "The Great Plan of Happiness," *Conference Report*, October 1993.
46   Smith, *Doctrines of Salvation*, 1:114–15.

Chapter Three

THE HELP MEET

SETTING THE STAGE FOR THE final scene of Creation makes the entry of Eve on the sixth day a surprising turn of events, especially if someone considers the woman a weak character susceptible to the wiles of Lucifer. Would God Almighty, who created the heavens and the earth and all things upon the earth, form a secondary character to tempt man as His culminating act of Creation, especially when "God saw every thing that he had made" and pronounced, "Behold, it was very good" (Genesis 1:31)? Was the woman Adam knew as "bone of my bones" a mistake in the creation process—flawed in character—or a deliberate act of God (Genesis 2:23)?[1]

We can fully understand Eve's story only when we know the events leading up to her appearance in the final act of Creation. With this in mind, let's look at the familiar story of God's creations.

"In the beginning God created the heaven and the earth" (Genesis 1:1; see also Abraham 4:1). Whether reading Genesis,

---

1   S. Kent Brown, "Approaches to the Pentateuch," in Kent P. Jackson and Robert L. Millet, *Studies in Scripture: Volume three, Genesis to 2 Samuel* (Salt Lake City: Deseret Book, 1989), 28.

Moses, or the Abraham account, the statement "God created the heaven and the earth" leaves "no room for the idea that the existence of life"—even the life of Eve—is accidental (Genesis 1:1[2]). While we may not know the details of the creation process, we are assured that God was not an absentee bystander. Of the Creation, the Prophet Joseph Smith said,

> You ask the learned doctors why they say the world was made out of nothing; and they will answer, "Doesn't the Bible say He *created* the world?" And they infer, from the word create, that it must have been made out of nothing. Now, the word create came from the [Hebrew] word *baurau* which does not mean to create out of nothing; it means to organize; the same as a man would organize materials and build a ship. Hence, we infer that God had materials to organize the world out of chaos—chaotic matter, which is element, and in which dwells all the glory. . . . The pure principles of element are principles which can never be destroyed; they may be organized and reorganized, but not destroyed. . . . They had no beginning, and can have no end.[3]

Brigham Young gave insight into the purpose of the Creation: "The whole object of the creation of this world is to exalt the intelligences that are placed upon it, that they may live, endure, and increase forever and ever."[4] Nothing in the statements of Joseph

---

2   Brown, "Approaches to the Pentateuch," 28.

3   Joseph Fielding Smith, comp., *Teachings of the Prophet Joseph Smith* (Salt Lake City: Deseret Book, 1961), 350–52.

4   Brigham Young, "Intelligence, etc.," *Journal of Discourses*, 7:290.

Smith or Brigham Young suggest negativity in the organization of this world or its purpose—to enable intelligences to live and increase forever. Also, there is nothing in the organization or purpose of the Creation to suggest that a vulnerable intelligence, subject to impulsive whims, would put a wrench in God's plan for man.

In fact, throughout the process of the Creation, God pronounced his works "good," meaning "perfect for the purpose for which God designed it."[5] Could it be that Eve was perfect for the purpose that God designed? The repetitive nature of the descriptive word *good* at the conclusion of each day or period of the Creation is characteristic of Hebrew literature in general. Instead of using exclamation marks to emphasis ideas or objects, ancient writers used repetitive words. The story of the Creation and the Garden of Eden is replete with repetitions of the word *good*.

The Creation of this world was staged in ordered periods of time pronounced "good."[6] In the Genesis and Moses accounts, the periods of time are called days, divided between morning and evening. (Never once does the word *noon* appear in the creation process.) The Apostle Peter stated, "One day is with the Lord as a thousand years, and a thousand years as one day" (2 Peter 3:8) Abraham recorded, "One revolution was a day unto the Lord, after his manner of reckoning, it being one thousand years according to the time appointed . . . this is the reckoning of the Lord's time, according to the reckoning of Kolob" (Abraham 3:4). "Whether termed a day, a time, or an age," President Russell M. Nelson said, "each phase was a period between two identifiable events—a division of eternity."[7]

---

5   Dummelow, *Commentary on the Holy Bible*, 4.
6   Nelson, "The Creation," *Conference Report*, April 2000.
7   Nelson, "The Creation," *Conference Report*, April 2000.

A Division of Eternity

In period one, "the earth was without form, and void; and darkness was upon the face of the deep" (Genesis 1:2; see also Moses 2:2, Abraham 4:2). The Lord said, "Let there be light: and there was light" (Genesis 1:3; see also Moses 2:3, Abraham 4:3). "And God saw the light, that it was good: and God divided the light from the darkness" (Genesis 1:4; see also Moses 2:4, Abraham. 4:4). The Lord "called the light Day, and the darkness he called Night" (Genesis 1:5; see also Moses 2:5, Abraham 4:5).

In period two, the Lord said, "Let there be a firmament in the midst of the waters, and let it divide the waters from the waters" (Genesis 1:6; see also Moses 2:6, Abraham 4:6). "And God made the firmament, and divided the waters which were under the firmament from the waters which were above the firmament: and it was so" (Genesis 1:7; see also Moses 2:7, Abraham 4:7). The Lord "called the firmament Heaven" (Genesis 1:8; see also Moses 2:8, Abraham 4:8).

In period three, the Lord said, "Let the waters under the heaven be gathered together unto one place, and let the dry land appear: and it was so" (Genesis 1:9; see also Moses 2:9, Abraham 4:9). The Lord called "the dry land Earth; and the gathering together of the waters called he Seas: and God saw that it was good" (Genesis 1:10; see also Moses 2:10, Abraham 4:10). The Lord then said, "Let the earth bring forth grass, the herb yielding seed, and the fruit tree yielding fruit after his kind, whose seed is in itself, upon the earth: and it was so" (Genesis 1:11; see also Moses 2:11, Abraham 4:11). In obedience to the word of God, "the earth brought forth grass, and herb yielding seed after his kind, and the tree yielding fruit, whose seed was in itself, after his kind: and God saw that it was good" (Genesis 1:12; see also Moses 2:12, Abraham 4:12).

Period four begins as the Lord says, "Let there be lights in the firmament of the heaven to divide the day from the night; and let them be for signs, and for seasons, and for days, and years" (Genesis 1:14; see also Moses 2:14, Abraham 4:14). "And let them be for lights in the firmament of the heaven to give light upon the earth: and it was so" (Genesis 1:15; see also Moses 2:15, Abraham 4:15). There were "two great lights; the greater light to rule the day, and the lesser light to rule the night: he made the stars also" (Genesis 1:16; see also Moses 2:16, Abraham 4:16). These lights were set "in the firmament of the heaven to give light upon the earth" (Genesis 1:17; see also Moses 2:17, Abraham 4:17). These lights were also "to rule over the day and over the night, and to divide the light from the darkness: and God saw that it was good" (Genesis 1:18; see also Moses 2:18, Abraham 4:17–18).

In period five, the Lord said, "Let the waters bring forth abundantly the moving creature that hath life, and fowl that may fly above the earth in the open firmament of heaven" (Genesis 1:20; see also Moses 2:20, Abraham 4:20). "And God created great whales, and every living creature that moveth, which the waters brought forth abundantly, after their kind, and every winged fowl after his kind" (Genesis 1:21; see also Moses 2:21, Abraham 4:21). The Lord blessed the living creatures and said, "Be fruitful, and multiply, and fill the waters in the seas, and let fowl multiply in the earth" (Genesis 1:22; see also Moses 2:22, Abraham 4:22). Period five stands out as the first time the Lord gave a command and a blessing to His creations.

With this backdrop, we now turn to the final period of Creation—the sixth period. "And God said, Let the earth bring forth the living creature after his kind, cattle, and creeping thing, and beast of the earth after his kind: and it was so" (Genesis 1:24; see also Moses 2:24, Abraham 4:24). "And God made the beast of the earth after his kind, and cattle after their kind, and every thing that creepeth upon the earth after his kind: and God saw that it was good" (Genesis 1:25; see also Moses 2:25, Abraham 4:25).

Instead of pronouncing a blessing on the beasts or other creatures—such as, "Be fruitful, and multiply," like God had pronounced on the creatures of the sea and the fowls of the air—the Lord said, "Let us make man in our image, after our likeness: and let them have dominion over the fish of the sea, and over the fowl of the air, and over the cattle, and over all the earth, and over every creeping thing that creepeth upon the earth" (Genesis 1:22, 26; see also Moses 2:22, 26, Abraham 4:22, 26). To whom was the Lord speaking when He said, "Let us make man" (Genesis 1:26)? The answer is found in Moses 2:26: "And I, God, said unto mine Only Begotten [Jesus the Christ], which was with me from the beginning: Let us make man in our image, after our likeness."

According to President Gordon B. Hinckley, this moment in the Creation was the beginning of God's "crowning creation"—the climax of the six creative periods.[8] This period was greater than the lights in the firmament, the seas, the trees, the fowls of the air, the beasts, or "every creeping thing that creepeth upon the earth" (Genesis 1:26). Yet these all needed to be in place before God formed man—"an event of such transcendent import . . . that neither heaven nor earth are ever thereafter the same."[9]

The creation of man was not a response to a divine utterance like "let the waters bring forth abundantly the moving creature that hath life." Instead, this creation called for the direct involvement of God the Father and His Son Jesus Christ. "So the Gods went down to organize man in their own image, in the image of the Gods to form they him," said President Russell M. Nelson.[10]

---

8 Gordon B. Hinckley, "The Women in Our Lives," *Conference Report*, October 2004.

9 Bruce R. McConkie, "Once or Twice in a Thousand Years," *Conference Report*, October 1975.

10 Nelson, "The Creation," *Conference Report*, April 2000.

"And the Lord God formed man of the dust of the ground, and breathed into his nostrils the breath of life; and man became a living soul" (Genesis 2:7; see also Moses 3:7, Abraham 5:7). Only to man did God give "the breath of life; and man became a living soul" (Genesis 2:7; see also Moses 3:7, Abraham 5:7). The elevated status of man in that single act is apparent. Yet it should be noted that God did not create the spirit of man. The Prophet Joseph Smith taught, "The spirit of man is not a created being; it existed from eternity, and will exist to eternity. . . . [When] God made a tabernacle and put a spirit into it, and it became a living soul. . . . It does not say in the Hebrew that God created the spirit of man. It says, 'God made man out of the earth, and put into him Adam's spirit, and so became a living body.'"[11]

Through further revelation to holy prophets, we also know that the first man was one of the sons of God. In premortal life, he was known as Michael, his name meaning "who is like God" (Bible Dictionary, "Michael"). In the war in heaven, Michael led the Lord's forces against Lucifer and, according to President Joseph Fielding Smith, "helped to form this earth. He labored with our Savior Jesus Christ."[12] And, of course, he was "appointed by God and Christ to be the mortal progenitor of the [human] race."[13]

The Prophet Joseph Smith taught that Michael, now known as Adam, held the keys of the dispensation of time "from generation to generation."[14] (A dispensation is "a period of time in which the Lord has at least one authorized servant on the earth who bears the

---

11 Smith, *History of the Church*, 3:387; Joseph Smith, "Character and Being of God, etc.," *Journal of Discourses*, 6:6.

12 Smith, *Doctrines of Salvation*, 1:75.

13 Mark E. Peterson, "Adam, the Archangel," *Conference Report*, April 1975.

14 Joseph Smith, "The Priesthood, etc.," *Journal of Discourses*, 6:237.

holy priesthood and the keys, and who has a divine commission to dispense the gospel to the inhabitants of the earth.")[15] With the prophet Daniel, Latter-day Saint prophets proclaim that Adam is the "Ancient of Days," and that at the close of the final dispensation he will meet the faithful in the valley of Adam-ondi-Ahman (see Daniel 7:9–22; D&C 116). There, Father Adam will present his "stewardship to Christ, his Master and his Savior, the Lord Jehovah, who in turn will give his accounting to the Heavenly and Eternal Father of us all."[16]

Although some debate whether Adam was the first man on this earth, in 1909 the First Presidency of The Church of Jesus Christ of Latter-day Saints took a decided stand:

> It is held by some that Adam was not the first man upon this earth, and that the original human being was a development from lower orders of the animal creation. These, however, are the theories of men. The word of the Lord declares that Adam was "the first man of all men" (Moses 1:34), and we are therefore in duty bound to regard him as the primal parent of our race. . . . Man began life as a human being, in the likeness of our Heavenly Father.[17]

As the first man, Adam was given *dominion*—meaning "rule" or "power"—over "the fish of the sea, and over the fowl of the air, and over the cattle, and over all the earth, and over every

---

15 *Bible Dictionary* "Dispensations."
16 Peterson, "Adam, the Archangel," *Conference Report*, October 1980.
17 "The Origin of Man, November 1909," in James R. Clark, *Messages of the First Presidency* (Salt Lake City: Bookcraft, 1970), 4:205.

creeping thing that creepeth upon the earth" (Genesis 1:26).[18] The responsibility given Adam was daunting. Considering the size of the earth and the broad scope of fishes, fowl, animals, and things that creep, the task would have been overwhelming for even an entire nation of men. But what is even more overwhelming was the *power of dominion* given to Adam. The power represents the absolute confidence and trust of the Lord in Adam, and it was a high point in the Creation.

Before scripture readers even have time to contemplate the magnitude of the responsibility and power given Adam, the scriptural text moves to the final scene of the Creation. The Genesis account begins as the Lord God says, "It is not good that the man should be alone; I will make him an help meet for him" (Genesis 2:18; see also Moses 3:18, Abraham 5:14). Knowing something of the heavy responsibility that weighed on Adam, the definition of *help meet* becomes all important. The word *help meet* is a noun based on the verb "to help." It means "one who helps," such as an assistant or subordinate to a master or superior.[19] In biblical tradition, the noun *helper* counters the oft-quoted meaning by introducing the concept of a trusted confidant one would look to in moments of distress. Take, for instance, Psalms 121:1–2: "From whence cometh my help. My help cometh from the Lord, which made heaven and earth."[20]

A Help Meet for Adam
Though Adam may have had many helps, such as food for nourishment and animals for comfort, these helps were not *meet*, meaning suitable for him.[21] There was no other creation in the

---

18 Eldred G. Smith, "Family Research," *Conference Report*, October 1975.
19 Meyers, *Discovering Eve*, 85.
20 Meyers, *Discovering Eve*, 85.
21 Dummelow, *Commentary on the Holy Bible*, 8.

image of God like Adam—no adequate companion, no "help meet." The all-wise Lord knew that a suitable help meet for Adam was a woman, not a man, who some might think would be the perfect choice because of his strength. But the Lord knew better.

Therefore, "the Lord God caused a deep sleep to fall upon Adam, and he slept: and he took one of his ribs, and closed up the flesh instead thereof" (Genesis 2:21; see also Moses 3:21, Abraham 5:15). The Genesis account reveals that from the rib the Lord created woman—in other words, the Lord used hard material ("the rib") to create the woman instead of using soft clay or dust, as was used to create Adam.[22] "The story of the rib, of course, is figurative," wrote President Spencer W. Kimball.[23] But if taken literally, President Russell M. Nelson stated, "Animals fashioned by our Creator, such as dogs and cats, have thirteen pairs of ribs, but the human being has one less with only twelve. I presume another bone could have been used."[24] President Nelson draws the allegory of "the rib, coming as it does from the side, seems to denote partnership. The rib signifies neither dominion nor subservience, but a lateral relationship as partners, to work and to live, side by side."[25]

Genesis Rabbah 80:5 tells of the Lord reasoning with Himself before creating the woman from Adam's rib:

> I will not create her from Adam's head, lest she be swell-headed; nor from the eye, lest she be a coquette; nor from the ear, lest she be an eavesdropper; nor from the mouth, lest she be a gossip;

---

22   Alter, *Genesis: Translation and Commentary*, 9.
23   Spencer W. Kimball, "Speaking Today: The Blessings and Responsibilities of Womanhood," *Ensign*, March 1976, 71.
24   Russell M. Nelson, "Lessons from Eve," *Conference Report*, October 1987.
25   Nelson, "Lessons from Eve," *Conference Report*, October 1987.

> nor from the heart, lest she be prone to jealousy; nor from the hand, lest she be light-fingered; nor from the foot, lest she be a gadabout; but from the modest part of man, for even when he stands naked, that part is covered.[26]

Regardless of whether the rib is figurative, literal, or allegorical, a woman was formed, and the Lord "brought her unto the man" (Genesis 2:22; see also Moses 3:22, Abraham 5:16). Adam recognized the woman immediately as "bone of my bones, and flesh of my flesh" and called her "Woman, because she was taken out of Man" (Genesis 2:23; see also Moses 3:23, Abraham 5:17).

The word *woman*, more of a generic designation than a formal name, literally means "man-ess"—being a form of the Hebrew word *ish* or *ishshah*.[27] The name Adam was now inclusive, implying a unity of two living souls—man and woman (see Genesis 5:2). But there was a distinct difference between the two souls. Although both man and woman were created in the image of God, Joseph Fielding Smith asks, "Is it not feasible to believe that female spirits were created in the image of a 'Mother in Heaven?'"[28] President Spencer W. Kimball taught, "God made man in his own image and certainly he made woman in the image of his wife-partner." President Kimball also taught, "You [women] are daughters of God. . . . You are made in the image of our heavenly Mother."[29]

---

[26] For the Genesis Rabbah 80:5, see James B. Hurley, "Man and Woman in Biblical Perspective," (Eugene, OR: Wipf and Stock, 2002), 74.

[27] Dummelow, *Commentary on the Holy Bible*, 8.

[28] Joseph Fielding Smith, *Answers to Gospel Questions* 5 vols. (Salt Lake City: Deseret Book, 2012), 3:144.

[29] *Teachings of Presidents of the Church: Spencer W. Kimball* (Salt Lake City: The Church of Jesus Christ of Latter-day Saints, 2006), 25.

In writing to the Corinthian Saints, the Apostle Paul made it clear that "neither is the man without the woman, neither the woman without the man, in the Lord" (1 Corinthians 11:11). The words of Paul suggest that Adam was incomplete before the creation of the woman. In other words, Adam was in a perfect state with Eve—a "oneness." Elder Charles Didier suggests the "oneness" was a sealing—a marriage:

> The first divine, righteous, ordained union between a man and a woman was sealed by these words, "A man . . . shall cleave unto his wife" (Gen. 2:24). This is the established doctrine, and it will never change. It is repeated in modern revelation: "Thou shalt love thy wife with all thy heart, and shalt cleave unto her and none else" (D&C 42:22).[30]

President Joseph F. Smith saw "oneness" as central to exaltation:

> No man can be saved and exalted in the kingdom of God without the woman, and no woman can reach perfection and exaltation in the kingdom of God, alone. . . . God instituted marriage in the beginning. He made man in His own image and likeness, male and female, and in their creation it was designed that they should be united together in sacred bonds of marriage, and one is not perfect without the other.[31]

---

30 Charles Didier, "Remember Your Covenants," *Conference Report*, April 1994.

31 Joseph F. Smith, *Conference Report*, April 1913.

This interpretation of "oneness" being a sealing—an eternal marriage—is consistent with *The Family: A Proclamation to the World*: "We, the First Presidency and the Council of the Twelve Apostles of The Church of Jesus Christ of Latter-day Saints, solemnly proclaim that marriage between a man and woman is ordained of God."[32]

Can it be assumed that Adam—a trusted warrior in the war in heaven, a helper in the Creation process, and the man who held dominion over all creatures upon the earth—would be given a woman in marriage who was sub-par or less than his equal? Would the woman have been a disinterested bystander in the premortal world as the valiant spirits risked their all to thwart Lucifer in his determined rebellious course against our Father in Heaven? Would she have been a fence-sitter easily diverted in discussions of the Creation and what it meant for the spirits awaiting their opportunity to come to earth? Would the woman have been reticent to accept the plan of salvation and Jesus as the atoning sacrifice? To Elder Richard G. Scott, "Michael who helped create the earth [was] a glorious, superb individual. Eve was his equal—a full, powerfully contributing partner."[33] Could it be possible to imagine any other scenario?

Adam and the woman were "both naked, the man and his wife, and were not ashamed" (Genesis 2:25; see also Moses 3:25, Abraham 5:19). The first commandment given to Adam and Eve was to "Be fruitful, and multiply" (Genesis 1:28; see also Moses 2:28, Abraham 4:28). That commandment is of key significance—"the very foundation of human life, of all society"—the

---

[32] The First Presidency and Council of the Twelve Apostles, *The Family: A Proclamation to the World* (Salt Lake City: The Church of Jesus Christ of Latter-day Saints, 1995).

[33] Richard G. Scott, "The Joy of Living the Great Plan of Happiness," *Conference Report*, October 1996.

family.[34] Adam and his wife were not commanded to spend their lives eating, drinking, and being merry (see 2 Nephi 28:7). They were commanded to "be fruitful, and multiply"—to be parents, for marriage is "the authorized channel through which premortal spirits enter mortality" (Genesis 1:28; see also Moses 2:28).[35] President Dallin H. Oaks said, "The power to create mortal life is the most exalted power God has given his children. Its use was mandated by God's first commandment."[36]

In addition to being fruitful and multiplying, Adam and Eve were commanded to "replenish the earth, and subdue it: and have dominion over the fish of the sea, and over the fowl of the air, and over every living thing that moveth upon the earth" (Genesis 1:28; see also Moses 2:28, Abraham 4:28). The later responsibility was obviously repetitious for Adam, for the Lord had given him the same instruction when he was a lone man in the garden. But by repeating the responsibility, the Lord was then also giving the assignment to the woman. The Lord told Adam and his wife, "I have given you every herb bearing seed, which is upon the face of all the earth, and every tree, in the which is the fruit of a tree yielding seed; to you it shall be for meat" (Genesis 1:29; see also Moses 2:29, Abraham 4:29).

The Lord then said, "And to every beast of the earth, and to every fowl of the air, and to every thing that creepeth upon the earth, wherein there is life, I have given every green herb for meat: and it was so" (Genesis 1:30; see also Moses 2:30, Abraham 4:30). And "God saw every thing that he had made, and, behold, it was very good. And the evening and the morning were the sixth day" (Genesis 1:31; see also Moses 2:31, Abraham. 4:31).

---

34 Boyd K. Packer, "Counsel to Young Men," *Conference Report*, April 2009.
35 David A. Bednar, "We Believe in Being Chaste," *Conference Report*, April 2013.
36 Dallin H. Oaks, "No Other Gods," *Conference Report*, October 2013.

"Thus the heavens and the earth were finished, and all the host of them" (Genesis 2:1; see also Moses 3:1, Abraham 5:1).

On the seventh day or seventh period the Lord rested "from all his work which he had made" (Genesis 2:2; see also Moses 3:2, Abraham 5:2). "And God blessed the seventh day, and sanctified it" (Genesis 2:3; see also Moses 3:3, Abraham 5:3). The word *sanctify* in Hebrew is *qadash*, which means "to consecrate or set apart."[37] On this holy day, the last in the Creation, the children of Israel were to remember the divine process of the Creation: "For in six days the Lord made heaven and earth, the sea, and all that in them is, and rested the seventh day: wherefore the Lord blessed the sabbath day, and hallowed it" (Exodus 20:11). On the Sabbath, the Creator invited the Israelites to be His partners in the renewal process of the Creation (see D&C 95:7; Exodus 20:8–11; Genesis 2:3; Exodus 31:17). Israelites accepted the proffered invitation by taming and molding nature six days a week, but on the Sabbath day, like the Great Creator, they hallowed the day by resting from their earthly labors.

Raphael Jospe explains, "During the six week days of productive work, people imposed their will upon nature. The Sabbath is to be a time when people refrain from creating changes in nature, and instead participate in [the] harmony of nature."[38] Resting from temporal cares gave place for the contemplation of concepts associated with the Sabbath—perfection, covenant-making, and completeness—all sacred concepts traced to the union of Adam and Eve on the sixth day of the Creation.

---

37 *Old Testament: Gospel Doctrine Teacher's Supplement*, 9.

38 Raphael Jospe, "Sabbath, Sabbatical and Jubilee: Jewish Ethical Perspectives," in Hans Ucko, ed., *The Jubilee Challenge, Utopia or Possibility?*" (Geneva: WCC Publications, 1997), 85.

Chapter Four

IN A GARDEN EASTWARD IN EDEN

THE STORY THAT HAS DEFINED Eve for centuries, of course, actually follows the seventh day of the Creation. The story unfolds in a garden planted by the Lord God eastward in Eden (see Genesis 2:8; Moses 3:8, Abraham 5:8). What would a garden look like that was planted by the Lord God (see Genesis 2:8)? No doubt it would have defied all description with its array of flowers, shrubbery, and trees.

Perhaps the Persian word *paradeisos*, meaning "an orchard," would best describe such a garden. In English, the best-suited word for such a garden is *paradise*. The Hebrew word *eden* means "fruitful" and "well-watered." The Babylonian word *edinu* means "steppe," "plain," and "parkland."[1] Putting together the various meanings of the phrase "Garden of Eden" suggests that Adam and Eve were placed in a delightful paradise, a parkland atmosphere—what Englishmen describe as "a King's pleasure park" and what Old Testament scholars write of as a "model temple (or temple replacement)."[2]

---

1   Dummelow, *Commentary on the Holy Bible*, 7.
2   Langer, *Remembering Eden*, 128.

Discovering the whereabouts of this pleasure park or model temple has intrigued scholars, theologians, and philosophers alike. Pointing to the Genesis reference of "a river went out of Eden to water the garden; and from thence it was parted, and became into four heads," with one head being Euphrates, scholars suggest the location of Eden was in Mesopotamia near the Euphrates River (see Genesis 2:14). Christians agree and suggest the Babylonian region as the logical site for the garden. Jewish tradition counters such notions by making a direct connection between "the temple in Jerusalem and the first spot of ground."[3] A famous passage from an early Jewish commentary reads:

> Just as the navel is found at the center of a human being, so the land of Israel is found at the center of the world. Jerusalem is at the center of the land of Israel, and the Temple is at the center of Jerusalem, the Holy of Holies is at the center of the Temple, the Ark is at the center of the Holy of Holies, and the Foundation Stone is in front of the Ark, which spot is the foundation of the world.[4]

Latter-day prophets disagree! They say that America is the cradle of the human race, with Jackson County, Missouri, the site of the Garden of Eden. "Joseph, the prophet, told me," said Brigham Young, "the Garden of Eden was in Jackson County, Missouri. . . . It is a pleasant thing to think of and to know where

---

3   John M. Lundquist, "The Common Temple Ideology of the Ancient Near East," in *The Temple in Antiquity: Ancient Records and Modern Perspectives. Volume Nine in the Religious Studies Monograph Series* (Provo, UT: Religious Studies Center, Brigham Young University, 1984), 65.

4   Lundquist, "The Common Temple Ideology of the Ancient Near East," in *The Temple in Antiquity*, 65; Midrash Tanhuma, Kedoshim, 10.

the Garden of Eden was. Did you ever think of it? I do not think many do." Brigham added, "In the beginning, after this earth was prepared for man, the Lord commenced his work upon what is now called the American continent, where the Garden of Eden was made."[5]

President Heber C. Kimball concurred with Brigham Young and wrote, "The spot chosen for the garden of Eden was Jackson County, in the State of Missouri, where Independence now stands; it was occupied in the morn of creation by Adam."[6] Believing the words of Brigham Young and Heber C. Kimball and "in accord with the revelations given to the Prophet Joseph Smith," Latter-day Saints profess "the Garden of Eden was on the American continent located where the City Zion, or the New Jerusalem, will be built."[7]

The Lord God invited Adam to "dress it" and "to keep," meaning to "cultivate" and "protect" the Garden of Eden (Genesis 2:15; see also Moses 3:15, Abraham 5:11).[8] It appears that Adam accepted the Lord's invitation to do that, for President J. Reuben Clark Jr. said, "Adam took her [the woman] . . . radiant and divinely fair, into the Garden he had dressed and kept for her, into the bridal home he had built, into the Garden that from then till

---

[5] Brigham Young, "Persecution—The Kingdom of God, etc.," *Journal of Discourses*, 8:195; See Journal History of the Church, March 15, 1857, 1, as cited in John A. Widtsoe, *Evidences and Reconciliations* (Salt Lake City: Deseret Book, 1960), 396.

[6] Heber C. Kimball, "Advancement of the Saints, etc.," *Journal of Discourses*, 10:235.

[7] See D&C 116; Smith, *History of the Church*, 3:35–36; Alvin R. Dyer, *The Refiner's Fire* (Salt Lake City: Deseret Book, 1969), 17–18; *Old Testament Student Manual: Genesis–2 Samuel* (Salt Lake City: Church Educational System, The Church of Jesus Christ of Latter-day Saints, 2003), 33.

[8] Dummelow, *Commentary on the Holy Bible*, 8.

now has been the symbol of heaven on earth."⁹ President Marion G. Romney added that in the garden, Adam and the woman were "worthy to enjoy—and they did enjoy—the society of God their Father. As a matter of fact, he visited them in the Garden of Eden and conversed with and instructed them. This instruction they needed because in their transition from spirits to souls the memories of their past experiences were blotted out."¹⁰

In the garden, Adam was taught the gospel of Jesus Christ, was baptized, and received the Holy Ghost (see Moses 6:51–68). There he and Eve knew no pain or sorrow. As immortals, they lived in a state of innocence for an undisclosed period of time. To be clear on their immortal state, Elder Orson Pratt wrote, "[God] did not make them mortal, but he made them immortal, like unto himself. If he had made them mortal, and subject to pain, there would have been some cause, among intelligent beings, to say that the Lord subjected man, without a cause, to afflictions, sorrows, death and mortality. But he could not do this; it was contrary to the nature of his attributes."¹¹

Two Trees in the Garden

"And out of the ground" of the Garden of Eden "made the Lord God to grow every tree that is pleasant to the sight, and good for food" (Genesis 2:9; see also Moses 3:9, Abraham 5:9). The aesthetic beauty of the trees and the nutrients in them to sustain life in the trees seems to be related. In Hebrew, the words *food* and *eat* are derived from the same root (*akl*). When used in the Genesis text, *food* and *eat* are actually repetitive. These two words

---

9 Quoted in A. Theodore Tuttle, "Altar, Tent, and Well," *Ensign*, January 1973.
10 Marion G. Romney, "Easter Thoughts," *Conference Report*, April 1975.
11 Orson Pratt, "Visions of Moses, etc.," *Journal of Discourses*, 21:289.

are used more frequently in the account of the Garden of Eden than any other word except *Adam*. The "striking repetition and placement carries its own message"—immortal life for Adam and Eve included partaking of food.[12] Trees in the Garden of Eden, including the fig tree, provided the opportunity for our first parents to partake of food.

The account of the garden moves quickly from food to two trees specifically identified "in the midst of the garden"—one tree bearing the food of eternal life and the other bearing the forbidden fruit of death. The first time the phrase "in the midst of the garden" appears in the Genesis text is in reference to the tree of life. The second time it appears is in reference to the tree of knowledge of good and evil (see Genesis 2:9; Genesis 3:3).[13]

The tree of life is mentioned at both the beginning and end of the account about the Garden of Eden and is only mentioned in four verses outside Genesis in the Old Testament. Each of the four citations is found in the book of Proverbs. Proverbs 3:18 states, "She is a tree of life to them that lay hold upon her: and happy is every one that retaineth her." Proverbs 13:12 states, "Hope deferred maketh the heart sick: but when the desire cometh, it is a tree of life" (see also Proverbs 11:30; Proverbs 15:4).[14] The final mention of the tree of life is in the last chapter of the book of Revelation: "In the midst of the street of it, and on either side of the river, was there the tree of life, which bare twelve manner of fruits, and yielded her fruit every month: and the leaves of the tree were for the healing of the nations" (Revelation 22:2). The meaning of this verse suggests that although the tree of life is "denied to man on this side of the grave, [the tree] will be found

---

12   Meyers, *Discovering Eve*, 89.
13   Mettinger, *The Eden Narrative*, 6.
14   Langer, *Remembering Eden*, 3.

by those who overcome in the conflict with evil, in the midst of the Paradise of God."[15]

Some biblical scholars suggest that the Genesis and Revelation references to the tree of life is a literary device in which similar material is placed at both the beginning and the end of a work, forming a sort of "frame" in Christian scripture.[16] Since mention of the tree of life appears in only a few verses outside the story of the Garden of Eden, other scholars suggest the significance of the tree is diminished to a secondary thought—or, even worse, an afterthought. The symbolic rhetoric of the tree of life in both Jewish and Christian tradition suggests otherwise. For example, the menorah, once housed in the temple at Jerusalem, is an "example of an Israelite transformation of the tree-of-life motif."[17] The twig that a "king or priest holds as his scepter" is a Christian symbol of the tree of life.[18]

Although there is much that could be said of the symbolism of the tree of life, the narrative about the Garden of Eden favors the other tree—the tree of knowledge of good and evil, which is essential to the development of the Adam and Eve story.[19] The second tree—the tree of knowledge of good and evil—renders the Garden of Eden not so idyllic. Why would the Lord, who "planted the garden eastward in Eden," place Adam, a man after his own image, in a garden with a tree that produced fruit containing seeds of death (Genesis 2:8; see also Moses 3:8, Abraham 5:8)? Is such an invitation indicated by anything in the Lord's warning, "But of the tree of the knowledge of good and evil, thou shalt not

---

15 Dummelow, *Commentary on the Holy Bible*, 11.
16 Langer, *Remembering Eden*, 34.
17 Lundquist, "The Common Temple Ideology for the Ancient Near East," in *The Temple in Antiquity*, 70.
18 Dummelow, *Commentary on the Holy Bible*, 7.
19 Mettinger, *The Eden Narrative*, 6.

eat of it: for in the day that thou eatest thereof thou shalt surely die"(Genesis 2:17; see also Moses 3:17, Abraham 5:13)?

The divine directive to Adam is a double-edged sword—or, as Doctrine and Covenants 33:1 states, a "two-edged sword," for it contains, "thou mayest" and "thou shalt not" (Genesis 2:16–17).[20] The command introduces in the garden scene the gift of agency offered to Adam and Eve. Liberty of choice—free will—is a precious yet perilous gift, for "it may be used either rightly or wrongly, and so there arises the possibility of temptation, of sin, of a 'fall.'"[21] With the right of choice comes the eternal principle of consequence, which the scriptures often illustrate with the word *if* followed by *then* (2 Nephi 1:9).

The principle of choice or agency is eternal; existing before the world was created, it is central to the Father's plan of salvation. Lucifer's rebellion against God the Father had everything to do with agency. Lucifer sought to destroy the agency of man, saying to the Father, "Behold, here am I, send me, I will be thy son, and I will redeem all mankind, that one soul shall not be lost, and surely I will do it; wherefore give me thine honor" (Moses 4:1).[22] Of Lucifer's rebellion, God the Father said, "Wherefore, because that Satan rebelled against me, and sought to destroy the agency of man, which I, the Lord God, had given him, and also, that I should give unto him mine own power; by the power of mine Only Begotten, I caused that he should be cast down" (Moses 4:3).

Lucifer in the Garden

As to where Lucifer enters the scene, look no further than the Garden of Eden—paradise, the temple model. He doesn't fit in

---

20 Reverend Derek Kidner, *Tyndale Old Testament Commentary—Genesis: An Introduction and Commentary* (London: IVP Academic Press, 1967), 61.
21 Dummelow, *Commentary on the Holy Bible*, 6, 8.
22 Dallin H. Oaks, "Opposition in All Things" *Ensign*, May 2016, 114–17.

the delightful paradise, except possibly near the tree of knowledge of good and evil. There, in the garden planted by the Lord God Himself, Lucifer found a home and became known as "Satan, yea, even the devil, the father of all lies" (Moses 4:4). Perhaps still smarting from his eternal banishment, once Satan was in Eden he was ready for "a frontal attack against the advent of truth."[23] His plan, laced with deceit and manipulation, was to separate Adam and Eve from God the Father. Satan knew who Adam was—the leader of the Lord's forces in the war in heaven. Satan also knew who Adam could become—the Ancient of Days. Satan understood the power of a united man and woman with God and the happiness and joy that comes from that unity. "Because he had fallen from heaven, and had become miserable forever," father Lehi taught, "[Satan] sought also the misery of all mankind," beginning with Adam (2 Nephi 2:18; see also 2 Nephi 2:27).[24] Satan knew the only way Adam and Eve could experience such misery was to hearken to his voice instead of to the voice of God (see Moses 4:4).

How many animals did Lucifer approach before he found "the heart of the serpent" leaned toward him? Of the serpent, the Genesis text states, "Now the serpent was more subtil than any beast of the field which the Lord God had made" (Genesis 3:1; see also Moses 4:5). The "subtle serpent" is not identified as Satan in the Genesis account, nor is Satan mentioned by name in the Old Testament until 1 Chronicles 21:1. The name of Satan appears in only thirteen verses in the ancient text, ten of those in the book of Job. The word *devil* is mentioned four times (Leviticus 17:7; Deuteronomy 32:17; 2 Chronicles 11:15; Psalms 106:37).

---

23 Marion G. Romney, "Satan—The Great Deceiver," *Conference Report*, April 1971.

24 Dallin H. Oaks, "Joy and Mercy," *Conference Report*, October 1991.

It is in the book of Moses account that the serpent is identified as Satan, who sought "to destroy the world" (Moses 4:6).

The narrative begins as the serpent approaches Eve. (There is no mention of the serpent approaching Adam with the tempting offer to partake of the forbidden fruit in either the Genesis text nor the book of Moses account.) The fact that the serpent is articulate is worthy of comment. The ancient historian Josephus wrote that before the Fall, "all living creatures had one language."[25] The serpent found Eve when she was alone. The very fact that Adam and Eve were not together has been fodder for Jewish legends that portray Adam and Eve often apart in the Garden of Eden, engaged in work or pursuing separate interests.

At first glance the interaction between the serpent and Eve appears an "unfortunate hour," for Eve made a life-altering decision without discussing the decision with Adam. Biblical scholars Marion Ann Taylor and Heather E. Weir lament, "O, fatal hour [when] by the mouth of the serpent," the woman was asked, "Yea, hath God said, Ye shall not eat of every tree of the garden?" (Genesis 3:1; see also Moses 4:7).[26] The satanic assault was an invitation for Eve to reevaluate the Lord's directive that "ye shall not eat of every tree of the garden" (Moses 4:7; see also Genesis 3:1). In the serpent's question—history's first recorded question—Lucifer introduces "the first recorded communication problem"—a lie.[27] In the lie, the serpent soon reveals himself as the father of all lies (see Moses 4:4).[28]

---

25 William Whiston, trans., *The New Complete Works of Josephus* (Grand Rapids, MI: Kregel Publications, 1999), 50.

26 Taylor and Weir, *Let Her Speak for Herself*, 26.

27 L. Lionel Kendrick, "Christlike Communications," *Conference Report*, October 1999.

28 Marion G. Romney, "We Believe in Being Honest," *Conference Report*, October 1976.

The lie should cause all honest seekers of truth to recoil, for ancient and modern scripture teaches "lying lips are [an] abomination to the Lord" (Proverbs 12:22) and "he that lieth and will not repent shall be cast out" (D&C 42:21). King Solomon declared, "Six things doth the Lord hate: yea, seven are an abomination unto him" (Proverbs 6:16). The first two things the Lord hates are "a proud look, [and] a lying tongue" (Proverbs 6:17)."[29] Hosea includes lying as one of five evil practices that will destroy Judah (see Hosea 4:2). The Apostle Paul counseled early Christians, "Wherefore putting away lying, speak every man truth with his neighbor" (Ephesians 4:25).[30] Most Christians recognize that to lie about a person—in this case the Lord God—is an expression of hatred, for "a lying tongue hateth those that are afflicted by it" (Proverbs 26:28). Through His Prophet Joseph Smith, the Lord said it more directly: "Thou shalt not lie; he that lieth and will not repent shall be cast out" (D&C 42:21). The inference of Lucifer being cast out is not lost on Latter-day Saints, who quote Jacob, the brother of Nephi: "Wo unto the liar, for he shall be thrust down to hell" (2 Nephi 9:34).

In the Genesis text, Eve does not hesitate to correct the serpent, as if in his question the serpent misunderstood the word of God. Eve said to the serpent, "We may eat of the fruit of the trees of the garden" (Genesis 3:2; see also Moses 4:8). In her statement, Eve acknowledged the serpent's words before informing him of the all-important exception: "But of the fruit of the tree which is in the midst of the garden, God hath said, Ye shall not eat of it, neither shall ye touch it, lest ye die" (Genesis 3:3; see also Moses 4:9). It is not known how much time had passed

---

29   Romney, "We Believe in Being Honest," *Conference Report*, October 1976.
30   Kendrick, "Christlike Communications," *Conference Report*, October 1999.

since the Lord told Adam and Eve about the tree of knowledge of good and evil, but there is no question that Eve had not forgotten the significant warning about the tree.

Bible scholar Harry R. Kissileff mused over whether Eve had eaten enough to satisfy herself the day the serpent approached her; if she had been satisfied, would she have expressed a continuing interest in conversing with the serpent? Kissileff concludes, "It is unlikely that she would have even listened to the serpent" if she were not hungry; he adds,

> Eve may simply not have eaten for a while and was therefore physiologically prepared to accept food. Physiological readiness to eat is essential in determining whether food is 'good to eat,' but the stimulus properties of the food are equally important. The modern nutritional industry is built on the premise that food can be manipulated to make it ever more acceptable, by increasing its visual and visceral appearance.[31]

Whatever the reason for Eve continuing to converse with the serpent, the tone of their conversation turns to debate as the "serpent grows bolder on seeing that the woman is willing to argue the matter."[32] In the spirit of defiance, "The serpent said unto the woman, Ye shall not surely die" (Genesis 3:4; see also Moses 4:10). The serpent's answer challenges the veracity of the penalty to be exacted for partaking of the forbidden fruit and sows discord between the woman and the Lord God by misrepresenting God's

---

31 Harry R. Kissileff, "The Apple and Eve: A Neuropsychological Interpretation (Genesis 2–3)," in Beth Kissileff, *Reading Genesis: Beginnings* (London: Bloomsbury, 2016), 29–30.

32 Dummelow, *Commentary on the Holy Bible*, 9.

character.[33] The satanic distortion of truth was an outright denial of the truthfulness of God's word.[34]

The seeds of doubt well sown in the serpent's heart "came from without," not from within Eve. This is an important distinction, for according to famed Bible scholar Reverend J. R. Dummelow, "Herein lies the hope of victory. The wrong approaches us from outside ourselves, and is not the native product of our own heart."[35] Reverend Dummelow concludes, "Our great security against [false judgments] consists in our being shocked at it. Eve gazed and reflected when she should have fled."[36] Reverend Derek Kidner put it this way: "Eve listened to a creature instead of the Creator."[37] As the serpent spoke of the precarious nature of God, he undermined the word of the Lord by depicting for Eve a downward path as leading to an upward status—"ye shall be as gods, knowing good and evil" (Genesis 3:5; see also Moses 4:11). President George Q. Cannon recognized in the serpent's words an element of truth that "when she should eat of the tree of knowledge of good and evil they should become as Gods," but cautioned that Lucifer "accompanied it with a lie as he always does. He never tells the complete truth."[38]

The Fall of Adam and Eve

"When the woman saw that the tree was good for food, and that it was pleasant to the eyes, and a tree to be desired to make one wise,

---

[33] Dummelow, *Commentary on the Holy Bible*, 9.

[34] Kidner, *Genesis: An Introduction and Commentary*, 68.

[35] Dummelow, *Commentary on the Holy Bible*, 8.

[36] Dummelow, *Commentary on the Holy Bible*, 9.

[37] Kidner, *Genesis: An Introduction and Commentary*, 68.

[38] George Q. Cannon, *Gospel Truth: Discourses and Writings of President George Q. Cannon. Selected, arranged, and edited by Jerreld L. Newquist* 2 vols. (Salt Lake City: Deseret Book, 1974), 1:16.

she took of the fruit thereof, and did eat" (Genesis 3:6; see also Moses 4:12). Experiencing no ill effects, Eve gave the forbidden fruit to "her husband . . . and he did eat" (Genesis 3:6). Thus came the Fall of Adam.[39]

For centuries, Christians and Jewish scholars have asked, "Was the fruit symbolic or was it literal? "Was partaking of the forbidden fruit an act of defiance against the word of God with sexual overtones?" Elder James E. Talmage answered the latter question with a clarion response:

> I take this occasion to raise my voice against the false interpretation of scripture, which has been adopted by certain people, and is current in their minds, and is referred to in a hushed and half-secret way, that the fall of man consisted in some offense against the laws of chastity and of virtue. Such a doctrine is an abomination. . . . The human race is not born of fornication. These bodies that are given unto us are given in the way that God has provided. . . . Our first parents were pure and noble, and when we pass behind the veil we shall perhaps learn something of their high estate.[40]

Did Adam and Eve feel remorse or sorrow over partaking of the forbidden fruit? In the book of Moses account, Eve says, "Were it not for our transgression we never should have had seed, and never should have known good and evil, and the joy of our redemption, and the eternal life which God giveth unto all the obedient" (Moses 5:11). In the book of Moses, Adam also

---

39 Alter, *Genesis: Translation and Commentary*, 11.
40 James E. Talmage, *Jesus the Christ* (Salt Lake City: Deseret News, 1915), 30; *Old Testament Student Manual*, 41.

voiced his gratitude: "Blessed be the name of God, for because of my transgression my eyes are opened, and in this life I shall have joy, and again in the flesh I shall see God" (Moses 5:10).[41] The words of Adam and Eve—"joy of our redemption," "eternal life," and "in this life I shall have joy"—do not sound like words of the remorseful, condemned, or damned (Moses 5:10–11).

Father Lehi explained the reason for Adam's and Eve's joy: "If Adam had not transgressed he would not have fallen, but he would have remained in the garden of Eden. And all things which were created must have remained in the same state in which they were after they were created; and they must have remained forever, and had no end" (2 Nephi 2:22).[42] President Brigham Young put it this way: "The Lord knew they would do this and he had designed that they should."[43] Brigham Young concluded, "We should never blame Mother Eve, not the least."[44] President Spencer W. Kimball said, "Mortal life is a privilege and a necessary step in eternal progression. Mother Eve understood that."[45] President Russell M. Nelson said, "We need women who have the courage and vision of our Mother Eve."[46] And President James E. Faust said,

> We all owe a great debt of gratitude to Eve. In the Garden of Eden, she and Adam were instructed

---

[41] James E. Faust, "What It Means to be a Daughter of God," *Conference Report*, October 1999.

[42] *Old Testament: Gospel Doctrine Teacher's Supplement*, 8.

[43] Brigham Young, "How to gain Eternal Life, etc.," *Journal of Discourses*, 10:103.

[44] Brigham Young, "The Lord's Supper, etc.," *Journal of Discourses*, 13:145.

[45] Spencer W. Kimball, "Privileges and Responsibilities of Sisters," *Conference Report*, October 1978.

[46] Russell M. Nelson, "A Plea to My Sisters," *Ensign*, November 2015, 95–97.

not to eat of the tree of the knowledge of good and evil. However, they were also reminded, "Thou mayest choose for thyself" (Moses 3:17). The choice was really between a continuation of their comfortable existence in Eden, where they would never progress, or a momentous exit into mortality with its opposites: pain, trials, and physical death in contrast to joy, growth, and the potential for eternal life.[47]

Finally President Dallin H. Oaks said, "It was Eve who first transgressed the limits of Eden in order to initiate the conditions of mortality. Her act, whatever its nature, was formally a transgression but eternally a glorious necessity to open the doorway toward eternal life."[48]

Given the account of events in Eden thus far, readers are poised to expect the dramatic—proof that the word of God was right that "in the day that thou eatest thereof thou shalt surely die" (Genesis 2:17; see also Moses 3:17, Abraham 5:13)—or proof that the words of the serpent were wrong when he said, "ye shall not surely die" (Genesis 3:4; see also Moses 4:10). For those anticipating that the forbidden fruit was laced with poison and that partaking of it would result in Eve's rapid death, such was not the case.[49] When there was no immediate ill effect, Eve gave the forbidden fruit "unto her husband with her; and he did eat" (Genesis 3:6; see also Moses 4:12). As to how long it took for the effects of the forbidden fruit to bring death to Adam and Eve, the length of Eve's life is unknown. As for Adam, a book of

---

[47] Faust, "What It Means to be a Daughter of God," *Conference Report*, October 1999.

[48] Oaks, "The Great Plan of Happiness," *Conference Report*, October 1993.

[49] Moberly, *Theology of the Book of Genesis*, 80.

genealogy (a book of remembrance) was kept (see Moses 6:8, 22). The book reveals that Adam lived 930 years before his death (see Moses 6:12).[50]

According to the Genesis text, however, there *was* an immediate result of partaking of the forbidden fruit—"the eyes of them both were opened, and they knew that they were naked" (Genesis 3:7; see also Moses 4:13). Conscious of their nakedness, Adam and Eve sought a covering. Another word for "covering" is *atonement*, which suggests a greater meaning for the word *naked*. The Hebrew word for *naked* is *erwah*, meaning "uncleanliness" and "shame." By partaking of the forbidden fruit, Adam and Eve were unclean and needed a covering—an atonement.

To hide their nakedness, our first parents "sewed fig leaves together, and made themselves aprons" (Genesis 3:7; see also Moses 4:13). An old Jewish tale speaks of all the trees in Eden shedding their leaves at the Fall of Adam except the fig tree, which was the tree of knowledge of good and evil.[51] Although the ancient story has little basis to draw on for a foundation, near the end of His mortal ministry, Jesus Christ, the Savior of the world, cursed the fig tree for being fruitless, alluding to the fruitlessness of Israel (see Mark 11:12–13, 20–22).

---

50 H. Donl Peterson, *Pearl of Great Price: A History and Commentary* (Salt Lake City: Deseret Book, 1987), 181.

51 Dummelow, *Commentary on the Holy Bible*, 9.

Chapter Five

THE VOICE OF THE LORD GOD

The aprons Adam and Eve fashioned provided a covering for their nakedness but were insufficient to hide our first parents from their Creator. Adam and Eve "heard the voice of the Lord God [as they were] walking in the garden in the cool of the day" (Genesis 3:8; see also Moses 4:14). By partaking of the forbidden fruit, Adam and Eve were vulnerable and fallen. Wearing only makeshift fig-leaf coverings, they sought to hide their shame from the Lord. To escape what surely would be divine judgment, "Adam and his wife hid themselves from the presence of the Lord God amongst the trees of the garden" (Genesis 3:8; see also Moses 4:14). In contrast, the Lord did not try to hide Himself from Adam and Eve—our first parents were the ones seeking cover. By partaking of the forbidden fruit, they chose to estrange themselves from their Creator, not vice versa (see Genesis 3:8; Moses 4:14). Therein lies the first fruits of their transgression.

When talking about Eve's actions in the garden, we are talking about transgression, not sin. "In a general sense and in most instances the terms sin and transgression are synonymous," wrote

Elder Bruce R. McConkie before making a distinction between the two terms: "There are situations, however, in which it is possible to transgress a law without committing a sin, as in the case of Adam and Eve in the Garden of Eden."[1] Due to their transgression, our first parents sought to hide themselves among the trees in the garden, much like a child hides from his parents in hopes of escaping the consequences of a wrong choice. The trees were not a good concealment, for it took only the questioning voice of God to bring Adam and Eve from their hiding place.

The Confessions

"And the Lord God called unto Adam, and said unto him, Where art thou?" (Genesis 3:9; see also Moses 4:15). The Lord knew that Adam and his wife were in hiding because of transgression. According to Elder Bruce R. McConkie, the Lord's question, "'Where art thou?' was an opportunity for Adam to consider the seriousness of his actions and to report to [the Lord]" (Genesis 3:9; Moses 4:15).[2] The Lord's question was meant to "draw rather than drive" Adam and his wife from their hiding place, much like the Lord's query of "why" to Saul and "what" to the Legion.[3]

"I heard thy voice in the garden, and I was afraid," Adam replied. He then confessed the reason for his fear—"because I was naked" (Genesis 3:10; see also Moses 4:16). There was a time in the Garden of Eden when Adam and Eve were "both naked, the man and his wife: and they were not ashamed" (Genesis 2:25; see also Moses 3:25). But that, of course, was *before* they partook of the forbidden fruit. This time, Adam was fearful, for he had transgressed the command of his Creator.

---

1   Bruce R. McConkie, *Mormon Doctrine* (Salt Lake City: Bookcraft, 1977), 804.
2   N. Eldon Tanner, "Where Art Thou?" *Conference Report*, October 1971.
3   Kidner, *Genesis: An Introduction and Commentary*, 70.

"Who told thee that thou wast naked?" the Lord asked. The correct and simple answer was that the serpent had told him, but the Lord's question went unanswered. The Lord then asked, "Hast thou eaten of the tree, whereof I commanded thee that thou shouldest not eat?" (Genesis 3:11; see also Moses 4:17). The question called for a simple "yes" or "no" response. When confronted in his fallen state, Adam presented facts that allowed him to pass the blame instead of giving the short but sure answer.

Adam replied to his Creator, "The woman whom thou gavest to be with me, she gave me of the tree, and I did eat" (Genesis 3:12; see also Moses 4:18). Where was Adam's delight in the woman he once called "bone of my bone and flesh of my flesh" (Genesis 2:23; see also Moses 3:23)? By answering "the woman thou gavest to be with me," Adam not only pointed the finger of blame at Eve, but also pointed it at his Creator—or, as scholar Robert Alter, wrote, "[Adam] passes the buck, not only blaming the woman for giving him the fruit but virtually blaming God for giving him the woman" (Genesis 3:12; see also Moses 4:18).[4] Rather than hide his nakedness and shame with fig leaves, Adam tried to cover himself with plausible excuses, thereby perhaps hoping to avoid the full impact of violating the Lord's command: "Of the tree of the knowledge of good and evil, thou shalt not eat" (Genesis 2:17; see also Moses 3:17).

"Adam's response was characteristic of a man who wants to be perceived as being as close to right as possible," said Elder Richard G. Scott.[5] Adam must not have known that he diminished himself in the very act of blaming his wife. Thereafter, the Fall of Adam and Eve has been known simply as the Fall of Adam. For example,

---

4   Moberly, *Theology of the Book of Genesis*, 84; Alter, *Genesis: Translation and Commentary*, 13.

5   Scott, "The Joy of Living the Great Plan of Happiness," *Conference Report*, October 1996.

Romans 5:12 states, "Wherefore, as by one man sin entered into the world, and death by sin; and so death passed upon all men, for that all have sinned."

The Lord next turned to Eve. "And the Lord God said unto the woman, What is this that thou hast done?" (Genesis 3:13; see also Moses 4:19). With the Lord's question, Eve was given the opportunity to give a straightforward response, such as "I did eat" (Genesis 3:13; see also Moses 4:19). Instead, like Adam before her, Eve stated a fact that cast blame on another: "And the woman said, The serpent beguiled me, and I did eat" (Genesis 3:13; see also Moses 4:19). The serpent didn't demand that Eve partake of the forbidden fruit; he beguiled her, offering assurance that in partaking of the fruit "ye shall not surely die" (Genesis 3:4; see also Moses 4:10). Eve made the choice to eat the fruit without compulsion—but when confronted by the Lord, she blamed the serpent.

Why would Eve, like Adam, seek to rationalize her choice? Elder L. Lionel Kendrick answered, "It has been from the beginning and it will be till the end that the natural man will have a tendency to rationalize and to blame his behaviors on others or on certain circumstances. When we attempt to place responsibility for our choices on others, blaming is an unrighteous form of communication."[6]

Judgment of the Serpent

The Lord God then turned to the serpent, the "prime mover in the transgression."[7] No questions were asked of the serpent in the Genesis text. In that scriptural account, the serpent was not given an opportunity to blame another or feign innocence. With a voice

---

6 L. Lionel Kendrick, "Christlike Communications," *Conference Report*, October 1988.

7 Dummelow, *Commentary on the Holy Bible*, 10.

of certain clarity and divine judgment, "The Lord God said unto the serpent, Because thou hast done this, thou art cursed above all cattle, and above every beast of the field; upon thy belly shalt thou go, and dust shalt thou eat all the days of thy life" (Genesis 3:14; see also Moses 4:20). The judgment pronounced upon the serpent was not condescending; instead, it was condemning. Lucifer, who had rebelled against authority in the premortal world, was condemned by that same authority to be "cursed above all cattle" (Genesis 3:14).

Whatever the serpent's stature had been before enticing Eve to partake of the forbidden fruit—whether tall or short, straight or bent—the serpent became the "basest of animals," physically repulsive.[8] God's judgment—"upon thy belly shalt thou go, and dust shalt thou eat all the days of thy life"—changed the physical stature of the serpent forever. No longer would the serpent appear as the most subtle of God's creatures. To be condemned to eat or "lick the dust" was a mark of degradation placed on the serpent (see Psalms 72:9; Isaiah 49:23).[9] No one, not even a serpent, could appear high and mighty when licking the dust for food.

The judgment upon the serpent was not complete nor would it be without an announcement of the plan of salvation with Jesus Christ at its core. The Lord said to the serpent, "I will put enmity between thee and the woman, and between thy seed and her seed; it shall bruise thy head, and thou shalt bruise his heel" (Genesis 3:15; see also Moses 4:21). Enmity, with all the friction and hostility that accompanies such strife, would now epitomize the relationship between the serpent and Eve and unborn generations. Evidence of such enmity can be found on nearly every page of the Old Testament—men fight against men, women and children suffer, and so on.

---

8 Aschkenasy, *Eve's Journey*, 45.
9 Dummelow, *Commentary on the Holy Bible*, 10.

There would be no peace or harmony between Satan and the woman or her offspring as long as time held sway. But this was not all. The Lord God pronounced the final blow upon the serpent: "It [the word in Hebrew is *He*] shall bruise thy head, and thou shalt bruise his heel" (Genesis 3:15; see also Moses 4:21). What appears at first glance the bruising of another's body was in actuality an announcement of the triumphal victory of Jesus Christ over the serpent.

Although it may appear odd that the victory of Christ over Satan would be announced in the Lord's judgment of the serpent, it is not odd. The placement of Christ in the judgment scene has much more to do with the redemption of God's authority than a direct promise to Adam and Eve—or, as Ezekiel 36:22 states, "Thus saith the Lord God; I do not this for your sakes . . . but for mine holy name's sake."[10] If there remains confusion, the Apostle Paul in his writings to the Romans adds clarity: "And the God of peace shall bruise Satan under your feet" (Romans 16:20). The implication of these scriptural passages is that while man and woman will suffer satanic bruises, the Savior Jesus Christ, as the "seed of the woman," will bruise the serpent's head.[11] In that pronouncement—the glorious pronouncement—the Lord God introduces Adam and Eve to the plan of salvation, a plan centered on the Atonement of Jesus Christ (see Alma 42:8).[12]

Within that plan is the doctrine that Jesus will come to earth to "ransom men from the temporal and spiritual death brought upon them by the fall of Adam."[13] Jesus will "satisfy the demands

---

10 Kidner, *Genesis: An Introduction and Commentary*, 70–71.

11 Dummelow, *Commentary on the Holy Bible*, 10.

12 Jay E. Jensen, "Keep an Eternal Perspective," *Conference Report*, April 2000.

13 Bruce R. McConkie, "Come, Know the Lord Jesus," *Conference Report*, April 1977.

of divine justice and bring mercy to the penitent." Jesus will be the Savior, Deliverer, Mediator, and Intercessor to "plead the cause of all those who believe" in Him.[14] Jesus will bring hope to the downtrodden, joy to the oppressed, peace to the weary, and salvation to the children of God.

Although the role of Jesus Christ is critical to the Father's plan, His name is not mentioned in the Lord's judgment of the serpent nor is it found within the pages of the Old Testament. Yet Jesus Christ, the Great Jehovah, is the God of the Old Testament, the Savior of the world. President Spencer W. Kimball explained:

> Old Testament prophets from Adam to Malachi are testifying of the divinity of the Lord Jesus Christ and our Heavenly Father. Jesus Christ was the God of the Old Testament, and it was He who conversed with Abraham and Moses. It was He who inspired Isaiah and Jeremiah; it was He who foretold through those chosen men the happenings of the future, even to the latest day and hour.[15]

President Joseph Fielding Smith testified, "It was Jehovah [Jesus Christ] who talked with Abraham, with Noah, Enoch, Moses and all the prophets. He is the God of Israel, the Holy One of Israel; the one who led that nation out of Egyptian bondage, and who gave and fulfilled the Law of Moses."[16]

On January 1, 2000, the First Presidency and the Quorum of the Twelve Apostles affirmed the above testimonies by writing,

---

14   McConkie, "Come, Know the Lord Jesus," *Conference Report*, April 1977.
15   Spencer W. Kimball, "Revelation: The Word of the Lord to His Prophets," *Conference Report*, April 1977.
16   Smith, *Doctrines of Salvation*, 1:27.

[Jesus Christ] was the Great Jehovah of the Old Testament, the Messiah of the New. Under the direction of His Father, He was the creator of the earth. . . . We solemnly testify that His life, which is central to all human history, neither began in Bethlehem nor concluded on Calvary. He was the Firstborn of the Father, the Only Begotten Son in the flesh, the Redeemer of the world. . . . We bear testimony as His duly ordained Apostles—that Jesus is the Living Christ, the immortal Son of God. He is the great King Immanuel, who stands today on the right hand of His Father. He is the light, the life, and the hope of the world. His way is the path that leads to happiness in this life and eternal life in the world to come. God be thanked for the matchless gift of His divine Son.[17]

Judgment of Eve

Although Eve's role in partaking of the forbidden fruit and giving the fruit to Adam is universally referred to as a "fall," the word *fall* does not appear in the Genesis account of the Garden of Eden. Yet the Lord God knew of Eve's actions and said in judgment, "I will greatly multiply thy sorrow and thy conception; in sorrow thou shalt bring forth children; and thy desire shall be to thy husband, and he shall rule over thee" (Genesis 3:16; see also Moses 4:22).

There are various biblical translations of the Lord's judgment of Eve. The Septuagint, a Greek translation of a Hebrew text, reads:

---

17   *The Living Christ: The Testimony of the Apostles, The Church of Jesus Christ of Latter-day Saints* (Salt Lake City: The Church of Jesus Christ of Latter-day Saints, April 2000).

"I will greatly multiply thy pains and thy moanings; In pain shall you bring forth children. And thy submission shall be to your husband, And he shall have authority over you." The Vulgate (Latin) translation of the Bible reads, "I will multiply your toils and your conceptions; in grief you will bear children, and you will be under the power of your husband, and he will rule over you."[18]

Whichever translation is used, the message to Eve is the same—sorrow in childbirth and submission to her husband, who has rule over her. Latter-day Saint leaders and women alike grapple with the divine judgment pronounced upon Eve. "I wonder if those who translated the Bible might have used the term *distress* instead of sorrow," President Spencer W. Kimball wrote. "It would mean much the same, except I think there is great gladness in most Latter-day Saint homes when there is to be a child there." As to the issue of "thy desire shall be to thy husband, and he shall rule over thee," President Kimball wrote, "I have a question about the word *rule* (Gen. 3:16; Moses 4:22). It gives the wrong impression. I would prefer to use the word *preside* because that's what he does. A righteous husband presides over his wife and family."[19]

In taking a closer look at both issues—sorrow in childbirth and the meaning behind the word *rule*—interpretations vary from condemning the woman who uses medicines to lessen the pain of childbirth to defining the word *rule* as complete submission of the woman to the will of her husband. These extreme renderings are rare but nonetheless troubling. No one disagrees that there is pain associated with childbirth or that the memories of that pain lessen when the beautiful baby is placed in the mother's arms. Few contend that the sorrow and pain of childbirth leaves lifelong, emotional scars. Yet, most agree that the anguish of losing a

---

18   Meyers, *Discovering Eve*, 95.
19   Kimball, "The Blessings and Responsibilities of Womanhood," *Ensign*, March 1976, 72; *Old Testament: Gospel Doctrine Teacher's Supplement*, 9.

newborn is slow to subside, as is the sorrow and pain of rearing a wayward child.

"To rule" comes from the Hebrew root *msl*. Biblical scholar Carol Meyers notes that "although the translation 'rule' is appropriate in nearly all of the more than eighty instances in which the verb is found in the Hebrew Bible, it would be a mistake to think that in each passage it indicates precisely the same thing about the kind of rule or control."[20] In the case of Eve, scholars Marion Ann Taylor and Heather E. Weir interpret the word *rule* to mean love: "Heaven never intended she should be ruled with a rod of iron; but drawn by the cords of the man, in the bonds of love."[21]

Elder Bruce C. Hafen added yet another possible dimension to the Lord's statement to Eve that "he [Adam] shall rule over thee" with the suggestion that "Adam shall rule *with* thee."[22] There is evidence for that possibility. In the Hebrew original of Genesis 3:16, the phrase "and he shall rule over thee" is *v'hu yimshal bakh*; the letter that begins the final word is *beth* (pronounced "batit"), and it may be translated "with." Could it be that the Lord was advising Eve that Adam "shall rule *with* thee?"

Latter-day Saints associate the word *rule* with priesthood, the authority to act in God's name. In the ideal marriage, the priesthood man presides within the marriage in righteousness. As President Boyd K. Packer said,

> We know that every father can, or should be, an officer in the priesthood, meaning that he holds the priesthood and presides over his family in righteousness. . . . We are sometimes charged

---

20 Meyers, *Discovering Eve*, 115.
21 Taylor and Weir, *Let Her Speak for Herself*, 27.
22 See Bruce C. Hafen, "Crossing Thresholds and Becoming Equal Partners," *Ensign*, August 2007, 27.

with being unkind to the sisters in that they do not hold the priesthood and therefore do not hold the offices that the brethren do. But it is well understood that whether or not we are exalted depends upon the sister who is at our side—the wife, the mother of our children—and no holder of the priesthood would in any way depreciate or mitigate the value and power of his wife. When I hear those comments that the sisters are less than the brethren, I wish that they could see inside the heart of every worthy holder of the priesthood and understand how he feels about his wife, the mother of his children—a reverence, not quite worship but a kind of worship, a respect for the companion in life that causes it to be that he can be exalted ultimately.[23]

Judgment of Adam

Was Adam cursed by the Lord because he listened to Eve and partook of the forbidden fruit? The Genesis text does not say that Adam was cursed: "And unto Adam [God] said, Because thou hast hearkened unto the voice of thy wife, and hast eaten of the tree, of which I commanded thee, saying, Thou shalt not eat of it: cursed is the ground for thy sake; in sorrow shalt thou eat of it all the days of thy life" (Genesis 3:17; see also Moses 4:23). The scriptural passage specifically says "cursed is the ground" (Genesis 3:17). It does not say "cursed is Adam."

The paradise that Adam dressed and kept was a far cry from "cursed is the ground" that will bring forth "thorns also and thistles"

---

23 Boyd K. Packer, "The Power of the Priesthood," *Conference Report*, April 2010.

(Genesis 3:17–18; see also Moses 4:23–24). Thorns and thistles are "signs of nature untamed and encroaching" and, as recorded in the Old Testament, they are signs of the Lord's judgment.[24] For example, Proverbs 24:31 reads, "It was all grown over with thorns, and nettles had covered the face thereof, and the stone wall thereof was broken down." Isaiah 34:13 reads, "Thorns shall come up in her palaces, nettles and brambles in the fortresses thereof: and it shall be an habitation of dragons, and a court for owls."

Presenting a vista of thorns and thistles is a foretaste or preview of what is to follow for Adam and Eve—a "verdict of banishment" from the Garden of Eden.[25] Another preview is learning "in the sweat of thy face shalt thou eat bread" (Genesis 3:19; see also Moses 4:25). None would deny that there had been an element of work in the Garden of Eden as Adam dressed and kept it, but work by "the sweat of thy face" was different (Genesis 3:19). "Work itself [is] not the legacy of the Fall" of Adam.[26] The legacy of the Fall is the toil required to bring forth necessities of life such as "the herb of the field" (Genesis 3:18; see also Moses 4:24).

Next, the Lord God pronounced that Adam would "return unto the ground; for out of it wast thou taken: for dust thou art, and unto dust shalt thou return" (Genesis 3:19; see also Moses 4:25). The phrase "dust thou art, and unto dust shalt thou return" is the most quoted verse in the Genesis account of Eden. It is common to hear this verse quoted at funerals and at graveside services. It is the promised fulfillment of the warning, "But of the tree of the knowledge of good and evil, thou shalt not eat of it: for in the day that thou eatest thereof thou shalt surely die" (Genesis 2:17; see also Moses 4:17). Physical death—the separation of the body from the spirit—was to be the lot of Adam and that

---

24 Kidner, *Genesis: An Introduction and Commentary*, 72.
25 Alter, *Genesis: Translation and Commentary*, 14.
26 Kidner, *Genesis: An Introduction and Commentary*, 35.

of generations to follow—or, as President Thomas S. Monson said, "Death is our universal heritage. All must pass its portals. Death claims the aged, the weary and worn. It visits the youth in the bloom of hope and the glory of expectation. Nor are little children kept beyond its grasp. In the words of the Apostle Paul, 'It is appointed unto men once to die'" (Hebrews 9:27).[27]

Adam, who would learn much of struggle and toil as he worked the unrewarding ground, learned that he would "be swallowed up in [the ground] and become part of it."[28] Mortality was the judgment "not only upon [Adam and Eve], but upon the whole earth and every living thing upon it, in the air, the waters, or on the face of the land," wrote President Joseph Fielding Smith. "Even the earth itself partook of the seeds of death. Since that day all living things, including the earth itself, have partaken of mortal existence."[29]

Hope in Jesus Christ

In the judgment scene in Eden, when all seemed lost and paradise forfeited, there came a newness, an anticipation, a hope. Its purposeful placement in the verse that immediately follows "for dust thou art, and unto dust shalt thou return," provides a startling contrast to the discouragement of death (Genesis 3:19; see also Moses 4:25).

The awakening of hope begins as Adam gives his wife a name: "And Adam called his wife's name Eve; because she was the mother of all living" (Genesis 3:20; see also Moses 4:26). "Mother of all living" does not resonate with thoughts of dust, despair, or permanent loss. "Mother of all living" seems an inappropriate name for the woman who had handed Adam the forbidden fruit and for the

---

27 Thomas S. Monson, "I Know That My Redeemer Lives!" *Conference Report*, April 2007.

28 Moberly, *Theology of the Book of Genesis*, 73.

29 Joseph Fielding Smith, *Answers to Gospel Questions* 5 vols. (Salt Lake City: Deseret Book, 1979), 5:7.

woman who had not borne children (Genesis 3:20; see also Moses 4:26). Yet it was the Lord's promise to Eve that her seed would triumph over the judgment of death. Jesus Christ, the son of God the Father, is the promised seed of the Mother of all living. Jesus will rescue and redeem all from the grasp of death and open wide the door of salvation through His atoning sacrifice.

The joys of deliverance through sacrifice may appear strange to billions of the Father's children, for large portions of the Old Testament say nothing about the Atonement of Jesus Christ. The word *atonement* means "to cover" and "to hide." It does not mean that shame (nakedness) no longer exists. It means that shame has been covered or covered over by the sacrifice of Christ. Anciently, Israelites celebrated the day of covering, known as the Day of Atonement (*Yom Kippur*). On that holy day, Israelites remembered that the Atonement covered the transgression of Adam and Eve—Eve, of whom the Talmudist wrote, "All women in comparison with Sarah are like monkeys in respect to men. But Sarah can no more be compared to Eve."[30]

The name *Eve* in Hebrew is *Havvah*, meaning "life giving."[31] Of the one hundred and twenty-six women mentioned by name in the Old Testament from Abigail to Zipporah, only one is named Eve, while eighty-four are named mother. According to John Hilton III and his wife, Lani Hilton, "On average, the Old Testament has one reference to mothers every 5.1 pages."[32] Mother or "one of its derivatives occurs 232 times in the Old Testament—50 percent more than all of the other standard works combined." Mother occurs

---

30 Carol Frogley Ellertson, "The Sanctifying Power of True Ritual Worship," in D. Kelly Ogden, Jared W. Ludlow, and Kerry Muhlestein, *Gospel of Jesus Christ in the Old Testament: The 38th Annual Sidney Sperry Symposium* (Provo, UT: BYU Religious Studies Center, 2009), 102.

31 Dummelow, *Commentary on the Holy Bible*, 10.

32 John Hilton III and Lani Hilton, "Motherhood in the Old Testament," in Ogden, Ludlow, and Muhlestein, *Gospel of Jesus Christ in the Old Testament*, 45.

ninety-six times in the New Testament, forty-one times in the Book of Mormon, six times in the Doctrine and Covenants, and nine in the Pearl of Great Price.[33] Although the name *Eve* appears only five times in the Bible, she stands alone among the women mentioned in scriptures, for she was the only one known as the Mother of all living, the matriarch of the human race.

Coats of Skins

The Lord God showed forth great mercy to Adam and to his wife, Eve, by making "coats of skins" in which to clothe them (Genesis 3:21; see also Moses 4:27). When the Lord approached Adam and Eve, they had only fig leaf aprons to cover their nakedness and shame. The Lord rejected this covering. He preferred garments of skins or sacred vestments, a similitude of the covering of the Savior's Atonement for the transgression of Adam and Eve. According to Old Testament scholar Shon Hopkin, "The symbolism of the coat of skins shows God's willingness to protect Adam and Eve (as the coat would do in the newly fallen world)."[34] The covering seems a simple gesture, but as Elder Bruce R. McConkie said,

> Now and then in a quiet garden, or amid the fires and thunders of Sinai, or inside a sepulchre that cannot be sealed, or in an upper room—almost always apart from the gaze of men and seldom known by more than a handful of people—the Lord intervenes in the affairs of men and manifests his will relative to their salvation.[35]

---

33 Hilton and Hilton, "Motherhood in the Old Testament," Ogden, Ludlow, and Muhlestein, *Gospel of Jesus Christ in the Old Testament*, 33.

34 Shon D. Hopkin, "Christ, Covenants, and the Caph," Ogden, Ludlow, and Muhlestein, *Gospel of Jesus Christ in the Old Testament*, 150.

35 McConkie, "Once or Twice in a Thousand Years," *Conference Report*, October 1975.

In the case of Adam and Eve, the covering was an assurance that God will intervene and rescue them from their fallen state. The coat of skins was symbolic of His abiding love. For that symbol, and what it means to the faithful, Latter-day Saints sing with the poet Charles H. Gabriel:

> I stand all amazed at the love Jesus offers me,
> Confused at the grace that so fully he proffers me.
> I tremble to know that for me he was crucified,
> That for me, a sinner, he suffered, he bled and died.
> Oh, it is wonderful that he should care for me
> Enough to die for me!
> Oh, it is wonderful, wonderful to me![36]

Cherubim

To further protect Adam and Eve, the Lord "placed at the east of the garden of Eden Cherubims, and a flaming sword which turned every way, to keep the way of the tree of life" (Genesis 3:24; see Moses 4:31). *Cherubim*, the plural of *Cherub*, are some of the more interesting creatures of the Lord. Elder Bruce R. McConkie wrote, "A cherub is an angel of some particular order or rank to whom specific duties and work are assigned."[37] The *New Smith Dictionary* describes cherubim as "heavenly beings whose forms were composites of such creatures as men, eagles, lions, and oxen" (see Ezekiel 1:5; Revelation 4:7).[38] Medieval cultures tried to mirror cherubim guarding the gate to Eden by placing images of supernatural guardians on entrances to holy places. By so doing, it appears those cultures understood the purpose of the cherubim was to bar access to "eternal time and

---

36   Charles H. Gabriel, "I Stand All Amazed," *Hymns* (Salt Lake City: The Church of Jesus Christ of Latter-day Saints, 1985), 193.

37   McConkie, *Mormon Doctrine*, 124.

38   William Smith, *New Smith's Bible Dictionary* (Garden City, NY: Doubleday, 1966), 63.

space, the mysterious, transcendent reality beyond the portal"— the metaphorical throne room of God.[39]

In every Old Testament passage in which a cherub appears, the cherub is an attendant of God. For example, in Psalms 18:10: "And he rode upon a cherub, and did fly: yea, he did fly upon the wings of the wind." In Ezekiel's visions, the cherubim appear as multi-formed throne bearers—"the likeness of four living creatures. And this was their appearance; they had the likeness of a man. And every one had four faces, and every one had four wings" (Ezekiel 1:5–6).

Drawings of cherubim adorned the innermost portion of the tabernacle in the wilderness. Embroidered depictions of cherubim on the veil of the Holy of Holies in the temple at Jerusalem were symbolic guardians (see Exodus 26:31; 1 Kings 6:23–25; Exodus 36:35; Exodus 37:7–9).[40] The fiery sword, which is not mentioned outside of the Genesis text, is a "suitable weapon to set alongside the formidable cherubim" to guard the tree of life so that Adam would not "put forth his hand, and take also of the tree of life, and eat, and live for ever" in his fallen state (Genesis 3:22).[41]

---

39 Langer, *Remembering Eden*, 129.

40 Kidner, *Genesis: An Introduction and Commentary*, 72–73.

41 Alter, *Genesis: Translation and Commentary*, 15.

Chapter Six

SHUT OUT FROM THE PRESENCE OF GOD

"Mortality without the dimension of temptation or trial would not be a full proving," said Elder Neal A. Maxwell. "It would be a school with soft credits and no hard courses."[1] There were no "soft credits" or easy courses for Adam or Eve in mortality, even though their partaking of the forbidden fruit was devoid of sin. Cain's sin of murder and the ill-advised behavior of other posterity members cannot be linked to "a parental model of sinful disobedience."[2] Adam and Eve transgressed in Eden, nothing more. Nonetheless, theirs was a fall—a fall from Eden and the presence of God.

The Genesis text reveals that the Lord "sent" Adam and Eve from the Garden of Eden (Genesis 3:23). The Moses account uses the word *drove* in conjunction with our first parents leaving the garden (Moses 4:31). Neither the Genesis nor Moses accounts say that Adam and Eve were "cast out" of the garden, a common

---

1 Neal A. Maxwell, *We Will Prove Them Herewith* (Salt Lake City: Deseret Book, 1982), 45.

2 James E. Faust, "The Supernal Gift of the Atonement," *Conference Report*, October 1988.

phrase used to describe their exile from Eden. Whether using the words sent or driven, the story of Adam and Eve moves to a mortal setting in a telestial world where our first parents were "shut out from [God's] presence" (Moses 5:4). There they faced "the full fury of mortality" with all its thorns and thistles.[3] With Eden behind them and thistles and thorns before them, mortality must surely have seemed bleak. By way of analogy, President Henry B. Eyring said,

> Almost all of us have seen a battlefield portrayed in a film or read the description in a story. Over the din of explosions and the shouts of soldiers, there comes a cry, "Man down!" When that cry sounds, faithful fellow soldiers will move toward the sound. Another soldier or a medic will ignore danger and move to the injured comrade. And the man down will know that help will come.[4]

Adam was the man down—fallen from paradise, the model temple, and the presence of his Creator. He needed help. His helper or help meet in the telestial setting was Eve, for as the Apostle Paul wrote to the Corinthians: "Neither is the man without the woman, neither the woman without the man, in the Lord" (1 Corinthians 11:11).[5] As Adam faced the consequence of the fall (mortality), Eve was at his side. When he tilled the earth in obedience to the Lord's command, Eve "did labor with

---

3   Dawn Hall Anderson and Susette Fletcher Green, ed., *Women in the Covenant of Grace: Talks Selected from the 1993 Women's Conference Sponsored by Brigham Young University and the Relief Society* (Salt Lake City: Deseret Book, 1994), 22.

4   Eyring, "Man Down!" *Conference Report*, April 2009.

5   Russell M. Nelson, "Lessons from Eve," *Conference Report*, October 1987.

him" (Moses 5:1). Like women in every age, Eve knew much of "in the sweat of thy face shalt thou eat bread" (Genesis 3:19; see also Moses 4:25).[6] Perhaps in recognition, appreciation, or love, Mark Twain wrote in his short story "Eve's Diary" of Adam standing at the graveside of his help meet saying, "Wherever she was, there was paradise."[7]

Yet outside of paradise, the story of Eve and her labors recedes into the background of biblical narrative. As Eve retreats from dialogue, philosophers, theologians, and scholars suggest her role in mortality was secondary to that of Adam's. They point to Adam's dominance on the pages of holy writ and Eve's lack of presence as one example of her fading importance. In contrast, President Henry B. Eyring quotes Ecclesiastes: "Two are better than one; because they have a good reward for their labour. For if they fall, the one will lift up his fellow: but woe to him that is alone when he falleth; for he hath not another to help him up."[8]

Motherhood for Eve

What the philosophers, theologians, and scholars fail to see is that Eve retreated from dialogue only to emerge anew in a role of great prominence—a role pronounced in the Garden of Eden when the Lord God spoke of "her seed" (Genesis 3:15; see also Moses 4:21). Eve, whose very name means "Mother of all living" (Gen 3:20; see Moses 4:26), became the matriarch of the human race. The Moses account says, "And Adam knew his wife, and she bare unto him sons and daughters and they began to multiply and to replenish the earth" (Moses 5:2).

---

6 H. Burke Peterson, "The Church Employment System," *Conference Report*, April 1976.

7 Mark Twain, "Eve's Diary," *Harper's Bazaar*, 1905; Jeffrey R. Holland, "Miracles of the Restoration," *Conference Report*, October 1994.

8 Eyring, "Man Down!" *Conference Report*, April 2009.

There is no aspect of Eve's mortal life that "compares with her divine appointment to be the vessel for the physical birth of a child who has been nurtured within her," said Elder David B. Haight.[9] The First Presidency said of the important role of motherhood: "Motherhood is near to divinity. It is the highest, holiest service to be assumed by mankind. It places her who honors its holy calling and service next to the angels."[10]

Biblical scholar Carol Meyers wrote of Eve's motherhood, "If ever there were a situation in which the condescending phrase 'only a wife and mother' should be expunged from descriptive language" it is in the case of Eve.[11] In mortality, Eve became "our glorious Mother" (D&C 138:39). In Elias L. T. Harrison's poetic hymn, "Sons of Michael, He Approaches," one verse celebrates Mother Eve:

> Mother of our generations,
> Glorious by great Michael's side,
> Take thy children's adoration;
> Endless with thy Lord preside;
> Lo, lo, to greet thee now advance,
> Thousands in the glorious dance![12]

"The sons and daughters of Adam began to divide two and two in the land, and to till the land, and to tend flocks, and they also begat sons and daughters" (Moses 5:3). And thus, the race of man moved on with Father Adam and Mother Eve standing in their rightful place at the beginning of mortality.

---

9   David B. Haight, "Woman as Mother," in *Woman* (Salt Lake City: Deseret Book, 1979), 14.

10 Message from the First Presidency, in *Conference Report*, October 1942.

11 Meyers, *Discovering Eve*, 139.

12 Bruce R. McConkie, "Eve and the Fall," in *Woman*, 67.

The Law of Sacrifice

There are several suppositions among Latter-day Saints as to where our first parents resided outside the Garden of Eden. A few suggest that Adam and Eve resided near the tranquil valley of Adam-ondi-Ahman in Daviess County, Missouri. Others place them near Far West on a grassy plain in Caldwell County, Missouri. Still others maintain that they resided in Jackson County, Missouri, clustered as near as possible to the Garden of Eden, as if longing for the day they could return to paradise.[13] No matter where Adam and Eve raised their children and tilled the ground, what is known for certain is they remembered Eden and their Creator and "called upon the name of the Lord" in supplication (Moses 5:4).

In response to their supplications, "they heard the voice of the Lord from the way toward the Garden of Eden, speaking unto them," but the Lord was not seen (Moses 5:4). No matter how many supplications were offered, Adam and Eve remained shut out from God's presence (see Moses 5:4). Yet, as indicated, they were not shut out from communicating with the Lord God. In the process of communication, Adam received a commandment. The commandment was not a two-edged sword—"thou mayest" . . . "thou shalt not"—as was the command in Eden in regards to the tree of life and the tree of knowledge of good and evil, nor did it need to be (Genesis 2:16–17). There was ample opposition in mortality and choices to make between good and evil. The Lord's command to fallen Adam was straightforward: "Worship the Lord their God, and should offer the firstlings of their flocks, for an offering unto the Lord" (Moses 5:5).

The command—the law of sacrifice—is a similitude of the great sacrifice of Jesus Christ for the redemption of mankind. The word *sacrifice* is drawn from two Latin words, *sacer* and *ficere*, which

---

13   See Dyer, *Refiner's Fire*, 114, 171.

mean "to make sacred" or "to make holy." There is no evidence in the Genesis text or the Moses account that Adam or Eve transgressed the command to sacrifice. On an altar Adam offered "the firstlings of their flocks" (Moses 5:5). His sacrificial offering was not a one-time event, for "after many days an angel of the Lord appeared unto Adam, saying: Why dost thou offer sacrifices unto the Lord?" (Moses 5:6). Adam's reply was as straightforward as the Lord's command: "And Adam said unto [the angel]: I know not, save the Lord commanded me" (Moses 5:6).

The angel said unto Adam, "This thing is a similitude of the sacrifice of the Only Begotten of the Father, which is full of grace and truth. Wherefore, thou shalt do all that thou doest in the name of the Son, and thou shalt repent and call upon God in the name of the Son forevermore" (Moses 5:7–8). The "forevermore" commandment—the first preaching of the gospel outside of Eden—served as a reminder to Adam and Eve and later to their "posterity that all mortals can be redeemed from the Fall through the Atonement of Jesus Christ."[14] Perhaps as a second witness, "in that day the Holy Ghost fell upon Adam, which beareth record of the Father and the Son, saying: I am the Only Begotten of the Father from the beginning, henceforth and forever, that as thou hast fallen thou mayest be redeemed, and all mankind, even as many as will" (Moses 5:9).

Adam rejoiced over the angelic pronouncement and "blessed God and was filled" (Moses 5:10). Being filled with the Holy Ghost, Adam prophesied "concerning all the families of the earth, saying: Blessed be the name of God, for because of my transgression my eyes are opened, and in this life I shall have joy, and again in the flesh I shall see God" (Moses 5:10). Eve was not one whit behind Adam in also expressing joy: "Were it not for our transgression we

---

14 *Old Testament: Gospel Doctrine Teacher's Supplement*, 15.

never should have had seed, and never should have known good and evil, and the joy of our redemption, and the eternal life which God giveth unto all the obedient" (Moses 5:11).

The Call to Repentance

Then like father Lehi, who had partaken of a fruit that had filled his "soul with exceedingly great joy," Adam and Eve sought ways to share the fruits of the gospel with their posterity and "made all things known unto their sons and their daughters" (1 Nephi 8:12; see also Moses 5:12). In so doing, says President Dallin H. Oaks, "Our first parents established the pattern, receiving a testimony from the Holy Ghost and then bearing witness of the Father and the Son to those around them."[15] Patriarch Eldred G. Smith mused over the unique opportunity of Adam and Eve's children to have two such exceptional preachers of the gospel: "They were well educated, having been taught by the Lord himself. What an education!"[16]

Adam and Eve not only taught the gospel of Jesus Christ to their posterity, they taught them "to read and write, having a language which was pure and undefiled" (Moses 6:6).[17] And there was a book of remembrance—a book of the generations of Adam—kept in the language of Adam and written "by the spirit of inspiration" (Moses 6:5). The book was a record of the beginning when "God created man, in the likeness of God made he him" and a record of holy men, like Adam, hearkening to "the voice of God" and calling on their wayward posterity to repent (Moses 6:1, 8).[18]

In the days of Adam and Eve, the call to repentance was largely ignored, even though Adam and Eve had "made all things known

---

15 Dallin H. Oaks, "Witnesses of Christ," *Conference Report*, October 1990.
16 Peterson, "Adam, the Archangel," *Conference Report*, October 1980.
17 Peterson, "Adam, the Archangel," *Conference Report*, October 1980.
18 Smith, "All May Share in Adam's Blessing," *Conference Report*, April 1971.

unto their sons and their daughters" (Moses 5:12).[19] President Marion G. Romney explained why: "From then until now, most men, like the first generation of Adam's posterity, have 'believed it not,' although God has repeatedly revealed it to all the prophets from Adam to Noah."[20]

As to why such disobedience against the Lord and His commandments took place, we need to remember that Satan, who had stood near the tree of knowledge of good and evil in Eden, had found a home in the world of mortality. His purpose, whether in paradise or mortality, was the same—to use lies to tempt and deceive those in the likeness of God. President Russell M. Nelson explained why such a grotesque figure, who was destined to eat dust "all the days of [his] life," could have such a powerful influence over the children of Adam and Eve by quoting Mosiah 3:19: "The natural man is an enemy to God, and has been from the fall of Adam, and will be, forever and ever, unless he yields to the enticings of the Holy Spirit, and putteth off the natural man and becometh a saint through the atonement of Christ."[21]

Perhaps finding it impossible to entice Adam or Eve in mortality, Satan turned to their children. The children had not walked and talked with God in the Garden of Eden, but surely they knew of their parents' experience. Yet when it came to hearkening to their parents' teachings, it appears that Satan's offer of enticing falsehoods was more appealing to some of the children of Adam and Eve. Satan came among the children saying, "Believe it not; and they believed it not, and they loved Satan more than God. And men began from that time forth

---

19   Smith, "All May Share in Adam's Blessing," *Conference Report*, April 1971.

20   Marion G. Romney, "Man—A Child of God," *Conference Report*, April 1973.

21   Russell M. Nelson, "Blessed Are the Peacemakers," *Conference Report*, October 2002.

to be carnal, sensual, and devilish" (Moses 5:13). Elder Bruce R. McConkie lamented, "Thus apostasy began; men fell away from the truth even in the day of righteous Adam; men turned to carnal and ungodly practices even in the day when there were living witnesses to tell them of Eden's beauty, of the fall and promised redemption, and of angelic ministrations and heavenly revelations of the mind and will of Him whose they and we are."[22]

The Story of Cain and Abel
Every parent knows something of the disappointments and sorrows faced by Adam and Eve in the rebellion of their children. The reaction of our first parents to the rebellion was to mourn before the Lord. Although mourning may not have given them what they hoped for as relatively few of their posterity hearkened to their words, "as many as believed in the Son [of God], and repented of their sins" were blessed—the Moses account pronouncing them "saved" (Moses 5:15). And "as many as believed not and repented not" were "damned" (Moses 5:15).

In looking for when the juxtaposition of "saved" and "damned" reached an apex in the lives of Adam and Eve, look to Cain for the answer: "And Adam knew Eve his wife; and she conceived, and bare Cain" (Genesis 4:1; see also Moses 5:16). The name *Cain* in Hebrew is *Kayin*, meaning "a spear."[23] Of Cain, Eve said, "I have gotten a man from the Lord; wherefore he may not reject his words" (Moses 5:16; see also Genesis 4:1). But like others, "Cain hearkened not" to his mother and father (Moses 5:16). The first recorded words of Cain were defiant: "Who is the Lord that I should know him?" (Moses 5:16). Not so with his brother Abel, who "hearkened unto the voice of the Lord" (Moses 5:17).

---

22 Bruce R. McConkie, *Mortal Messiah: From Bethlehem to Calvary,* Book IV (Salt Lake City: Deseret Book, 1981), 1:229–30.
23 Dummelow, *Commentary on the Holy Bible,* 11.

The story of Cain and Abel is the first recorded instance of "a negative exemplification of the double love commandment, a failure to love God and love neighbor."[24] Satan commanded Cain to "make an offering unto the Lord" (Moses 5:18); at first reading, that command does not appear satanic. It appears repetitive of the Lord's command to "offer the firstlings of their flock, for an offering unto the Lord" (Moses 5:5). But Satan was surely not wanting Cain to fulfill the Lord's command.

"In process of time it came to pass that Cain brought of the fruit of the ground an offering unto the Lord" (Moses 5:19; see also Genesis 4:3). Fruit wasn't a creative way of fulfilling the Lord's command; it was an affront to God because of the way in which it was offered. Abel, like Father Adam before him, brought as an offering "firstlings of his flock, and of the fat thereof. And the Lord had respect unto Abel and to his offering" (Genesis 4:4; see also Moses 5:20). Of these two very different offerings, the Prophet Joseph Smith said, "Abel offered to God a sacrifice that was accepted, which was the firstlings of the flock. Cain offered the fruit of the ground, and was not accepted, because he could not do it in faith."[25]

Rather than repent and then present a faithful offering to the Lord, Cain became "very wroth," meaning "intensely angry" and "highly incensed," and "his countenance fell" (Genesis 4:5; see also Moses 5:21). The Lord asked Cain, "Why art thou wroth? And why is thy countenance fallen?" (Genesis 4:6; see also Moses 5:22). Without waiting for a response, the Lord assured Cain, "If thou doest well, shalt thou not be accepted?" (Genesis 4:7).

The encounter between the Lord and Cain was not a rivalry between the herdsman Abel and the farmer Cain. It was an encounter between the Lord God and Cain that centered on the possible

---

24 Moberly, *Theology of the Book of Genesis*, 88.
25 Smith, *Teachings of the Prophet Joseph Smith*, 58.

displacement of an older brother for the younger brother if Cain did not repent, for "sin lieth at the door" (Genesis 4:7; see also Moses 5:23). Sin and all that leads to it engulfed Cain, who "listened not any more to the voice of the Lord, neither to Abel, his brother, who walked in holiness before the Lord" (Moses 5:26). In wrath, Cain slew his brother and entered into an unholy alliance with Satan, becoming known as "Mahan, the master of this great secret, that I may murder and get gain" (Moses 5:31). Cain gloried in his wickedness, "saying: I am free; surely the flocks of my brother falleth into my hands" (Moses 5:33).

For Adam and Eve there was no glory in what Cain had done. In sorrow, they "mourned before the Lord" (Moses 5:27). Their mourning was in direct contrast to Eve's words at the birth of Cain: "I have gotten a man from the Lord; wherefore he may not reject his words" (Moses 5:16; see also Genesis 4:1). Cain's rejection of the word of the Lord and his murderous act was the triumph of evil in a bitter conflict over an offering to the Lord.[26]

"Where is Abel, thy brother?" the Lord asked of Cain (Genesis 4:9; see also Moses 5:34). Cain lied in his response: "I know not" (Genesis 4:9; see also Moses 5:34). Cain then asked God, "Am I my brother's keeper?" (Genesis 4:9; see also Moses 5:34). Besides his depth of depravity, Cain's "impudent denial that he [had] harmed Abel" and his refusal to accept responsibility for his brother's life is the opposite of a confession.[27] Unmoved by Cain's denial, the Lord passed judgment on him: "For from this time forth thou shalt be the father of his lies; thou shalt be called Perdition . . . And it shall be said in time to come—That these abominations were had from Cain; for he rejected the greater counsel which was had from God; and this is a cursing which I will put upon thee, except thou repent" (Moses 5:24–25).

---

26   N. Eldon Tanner, "Where Art Thou?" *Conference Report*, October 1971.
27   Dummelow, *Commentary on the Holy Bible*, 11.

The Final Chapter in Eve's Story

As Cain's repentance was not forthcoming, our story returns to his mourning parents, who continued to supplicate the Lord and offer sacrifices upon an altar. "And Adam knew his wife again; and she bare a son, and called his name Seth: For God, said she, hath appointed me another seed instead of Abel, whom Cain slew" (Genesis 4:25; see also Moses 6:2).

Following Seth's birth, Eve disappears from the pages of the Old Testament. Was her life extended 930 years like that of Adam? Did she bear other sons or daughters? Why was she "hidden behind the cultural legacy of a male-dominated society?"[28] Many questions swirl around the final chapters of Eve's story. At age sixteen, Emily Dickinson wrote to a friend: "I have lately come to the conclusion that I am Eve, alias Mrs. Adam. You know there is no account of her death in the Bible, and why am not I Eve? If you find any statements which you think likely to prove the truth of the case, I wish you would send them to me without delay."[29] Although the Dickinson suggestion is preposterous, there are people all across the earth who still wonder what happened to Eve.

The remainder of Eve's story is unknown. However, the story of her last-born son *is* known. "Seth was a perfect man, and his likeness was the express likeness of his father [Adam], insomuch that he seemed to be like unto his father in all things, and could be distinguished from him only by his age" (D&C 107:43). John Taylor said of Seth, "[He] inherited the priesthood and promises of his

---

28 Meyers, *Discovering Eve*, 189.
29 Emily E. Dickenson to Mrs. Strong, January 12, 1846, as cited in Mabel Loomis Todd, ed., *The Letters of Emily Dickinson, 1845–1886* (Boston: Little, Brown, and Company, 1906), 18.

martyred brother [Abel]."[30] At age sixty-nine Seth received the holy priesthood from the hands of his father, Adam, and was promised that "his posterity should be the chosen of the Lord, and that they should be preserved unto the end of the earth" (D&C 107:42). The promises given to Seth were later extended to his descendant Abraham.[31] Patriarch Eldred G. Smith said of the promises,

> Hence, all nations and families of the earth may receive the blessings of the gospel and eternal life through their faithfulness. To fulfill this promise given to Adam, then, the necessity is apparent of a renewing of priesthood leadership through a prophet of God at various intervals throughout time. These intervals have been called dispensations: from Adam to Seth—to Enoch—to Noah—to Abraham—to Moses—to Elias (Elijah)—to John the Baptist—to Jesus Christ—to the apostles Peter, James, and John.[32]

Conclusion

Eve was the last of God's creations in this world, and, as President Gordon B. Hinckley said, she was "The grand summation of all the work that had gone before."[33]

"Eve is a joint-participant with Adam in all his ministry," wrote Elder Bruce R. McConkie, "and will inherit jointly with him all the

---

30 John Taylor, *Mediation and Atonement of Our Lord and Savior Jesus Christ* (Salt Lake City: Deseret News, 1882), 67.

31 Eldred G. Smith, "All May Share in Adam's Blessing," *Conference Report*, April 1971.

32 Smith, "All May Share in Adam's Blessing," *Conference Report*, April 1971.

33 Hinckley, "The Women in Our Lives," *Conference Report*, October 2004.

blessings appertaining to his ministry, and will inherit jointly with him all the blessings appertaining to his high state of exaltation."[34]

When a "thousand thousands" shall minister unto Adam, and before whom "ten thousand times ten thousand" shall stand in a day of judgment, it is likely that these same crowds will express appreciation and adoration to Adam's help meet, Eve (Dan. 7:10).[35] After all, Eve played a vital role in the plan of salvation—or, as Elder Boyd K. Packer said, "Events from the Creation to the final, winding-up scene are not based on *chance*; they are based on *choice!* Had there been no Creation, no Fall, there should have been no need for any Atonement, neither a Redeemer to mediate for us."[36] Likewise, if there had been no Eve, where would we turn to find another matriarch of the human race? Where would we look to find a help meet for Adam, a wife, an eternal companion? Where would we find a marriage of two such noble souls in paradise?

W. W. Phelps wrote the following:

"The Marriage"
When earth was dress'd in beauty,
And join'd with heaven above,
The Lord took Eve to Adam,
And taught them how to love.

. . . . . .

And bless'd them at an altar,
For chaste and pure desire,
That no unhallowed being
Might offer there "Strange fire."

---

34 McConkie, *Mormon Doctrine*, 176.
35 McConkie, "Eve and the Fall," in *Woman*, 68.
36 Boyd K. Packer, "Atonement, Agency, Accountability," *Conference Report*, April 1988.

. . . . . .

Beware of all temptation;
Be good, be just, be wise,
Be even as the angels,
That dwell in Paradise.

. . . . . .

Go multiply,—replenish,
And fill the earth with men,
That all your vast creation,
May come to God again:—

. . . . . .

And dwell amid perfection,
In Zion's wide domains,
Where union is eternal,
And Jesus ever reigns.[37]

Phelps expresses appreciation for Mother Eve, whose choice made it possible for me to live—not just live in mortality. Because of "her seed," I can live with my Father in Heaven. Because of the choice of Adam and Eve to transgress, our first parents were sent from paradise to "[bring] forth children; yea, even the family of all the earth" (2 Nephi 2:20). This was not done in rebellion to God, for "all things have been done in the wisdom of him who knoweth all things. Adam [and Eve] fell that men might be; and men are, that they might have joy" (2 Nephi 2:24–25).

I joy in proclaiming Mother Eve as exemplar of womanhood. Eve labored with her husband, Adam, to till the ground. She supplicated the Lord for divine guidance. She bore children and

---

37 Michael Hicks, *Mormonism and Music: A History* (Urbana and Chicago: University of Illinois, 1989), 22.

taught them the gospel of Jesus Christ and the plan of salvation. How could such a woman be faulted generation after generation?

Elder James E. Talmage lamented that "it has become a common practice with mankind to heap reproaches upon the progenitors of the family, and to picture the supposedly blessed state in which we would be living but for the fall." Elder Talmage concluded his remarks with words of rebuttal for those who minimize the important choice of Adam and Eve: "Our first parents are entitled to our deepest gratitude for their legacy to posterity—the means of winning title to glory, exaltation and eternal lives."[38] To this I testify.

---

38 James E. Talmage, *The Articles of Faith* (Salt Lake City: The Church of Jesus Christ of Latter-day Saints, 1960), 70.

About the Author

DR. SUSAN EASTON BLACK JOINED the faculty of Brigham Young University in 1978 and taught Church history and doctrine until she retired to serve multiple missions with her husband, George Durrant. She is also past associate dean of general education and honors and director of Church history in the Religious Studies Center.

The recipient of numerous academic awards, she received the Karl G. Maeser Distinguished Faculty Lecturer Award in 2000, the highest award given a professor on the BYU Provo campus. Susan has authored, edited, and compiled more than 100 books and 250 articles.